P9-EMH-023

THE LIBRARY OF AFRICAN-AMERICAN BIOGRAPHY

John David Smith, editor

Walter White

Walter White

THE DILEMMA OF
BLACK IDENTITY IN AMERICA

Thomas Dyja

*The Library of
African-American Biography*

IVAN R. DEE · CHICAGO

www.ivanrdee.com

Library of Congress Cataloging-in-Publication Data:
Dyja, Tom.
  Walter White : the dilemma of Black identity in America / Thomas Dyja.
      p. cm.
  Includes bibliographical references and index.
  ISBN-13: 978-1-56663-766-4 (cloth : alk. paper)
  ISBN-10: 1-56663-766-X (cloth : alk. paper)
    1. White, Walter Francis, 1893–1955. 2. African Americans—Biography.
  3. National Association for the Advancement of Colored People—
  Biography. 4. African American civil rights workers—Biography. 5. Civil
  rights movements—United States—History—20th century. 6. African
  Americans—Civil rights—History—20th century. 7. United States—
  Race relations—History—20th century. 8. African American novelists—
  Biography. 9. African Americans—Intellectual life—20th century.
  10. African Americans—Race identity—Case studies. I. Title.
  E185.97.W6D95 2008
  323.092—dc22
  [B]   2008019753

For Thelma

Contents

Walter White

Prologue

MORE THAN FIFTY YEARS after his death, Walter White still makes people uncomfortable. Despite an incredible, Zelig-like presence in thirty years of American history, and international fame in his lifetime, he's virtually unknown today, first because his life begs the unsettling question of what, exactly, makes a person white or black in America. W. E. B. Du Bois's dismissive construction that black is having to ride Jim Crow through Georgia may have been definition enough for many in the 1930s, but it fails to encompass the full dimensions of black life in America and the world in which White grew up. "Legally" black, White was, to all appearances, Caucasian, with blond hair and blue eyes and sharp features. People still question whether he was actually black, even though he was raised black, among a family and a community that considered themselves black, and worked tirelessly for the cultural and legal advancement of African Americans. Those historians who do not entirely overlook him tend to view White's every action, public and private, through the lens of his fair complexion. But our readings of White, who had no doubts about his racial identity, often say more about us than about the man himself.

White was never a "tragic mulatto," a victim of his ambiguous skin. Instead, for thirty-five years he made the most of it and became the nation's leading spokesman for African Americans, confounding, profiting, and saving lives with his unexpected identity. As a young investigator for the NAACP and then as a lobbyist, he, more than any other one person, was responsible for turning Americans against lynching. As a literary figure, he not only wrote one of the first novels of the Harlem Renaissance but provided much of the connective energy that made that whole scene possible. In 1931 he became secretary of the NAACP, managing to keep the organization alive during the depression, nurturing and promoting the Legal Defense and Education Fund so it could pursue the strategy ultimately leading to *Brown v. Board of Education*. He led the first successful public challenge of a Supreme Court nominee, and lobbied Hollywood for better roles and representations for black America. Through his friendship with Eleanor Roosevelt, he put civil rights on the national agenda for the first time, only to be forced by the politics of the cold war into a false choice between domestic advancement through anti-communism, or the cause of anti-colonialism. His life bridged the coming of Jim Crow and the modern era of civil rights; his work permitted the mass movements of the fifties and sixties to march on a paved road of legal precedent. Full of a bounding, salesman's energy, constantly merging his own self-interests with those of the civil rights movement, White was as much about the noise he made as the accomplishments that he was truly responsible for.

The inspiration and brilliance of Du Bois allow many to excuse his embrace of Stalinism and Mao, and a personality and private life no less thorny than White's. Yet the volume and importance of White's practical achievements, when not ignored, tend to come wrapped in ideology as the work of a schemer or someone less than serious. The following pages are by no means intended as hagiography—White was no saint—but I have tried not to assign moral superiority to received wisdom, and to avoid notions of history from left and right that serve theory more than they illuminate the realities of America during three complex and pivotal decades. To understand White, we must risk feeling uncomfortable about more than just race, and confront some very essential questions. Do the ends always justify the means? Is bottom-up change somehow better than change from the top? How much should one compromise on principle? Can a loyal friend, a champion of good, be a cold husband and father?

There are no easy answers to such questions, at least in the real world, and admitting White's existence does not require our approval of him. But the choices he made that ultimately locked away his legacy were not choices between the black race and the white race; they were between the black race and Walter White, the man. His rise, immense success, and ultimate oblivion is, in the end, a story about choices we all make, regardless of race.

White dreamed of a nation that judged all its citizens on their own merits, no matter their color. Restoring him to his place in the story of the African-American struggle fills the void between Booker T. Washington and Dr. Martin Luther King, Jr., and further clarifies the vision of the modern civil rights movement as the culmination of generations of work and philosophy—the final sounding of the trumpets around Jericho, not the first. By the sixties he was considered someone to be forgotten, a symbol of everything the new activism wanted to get past. But all these years later, we still haven't caught up to his dreams.

CHAPTER ONE

A World of His Own

✍ In the waning sun of September 18, 1895, Booker T. Washington, a former slave and founder of the Tuskegee Institute, rose before the Cotton States and International Exposition in Atlanta's Piedmont Park with an offer for white America. Convinced that wealth, not legislation, was the way to survival and success for African Americans, Washington took it upon himself to tell the well-heeled white Southern businessmen sitting before him that if only white America would let them pursue that wealth unmolested, black America would accept segregation.

Whites, especially in the South, applauded the "Atlanta Compromise" with something close to euphoria; social equality was now off the table, and white power would remain unchallenged. Blacks, though hardly unanimous in their support of the Wizard of Tuskegee, warily played along if it meant safety and stability—there'd been more than one thousand reported lynchings in America since 1890. Even W. E. B. Du Bois, soon to be Washington's nemesis, praised the speech. A year later the Supreme Court found in *Plessy v. Ferguson* that separate but equal accommodations were legal under the Constitution. With these two moments— Washington's Atlanta Compromise and *Plessy*—a bleak and destructive period in American history began. From 1896 until 1954, America watched as Southern states systematically denied millions of African Americans the political, economic, and social rights they'd finally received during Reconstruction. Jim Crow, a campaign of precise "legal" dehumanization that might very well have served as a model for Nazi Germany, came to rule every corner of Southern life.

Black skilled tradesmen—masons, blacksmiths, and carpenters—found their white clientele suddenly turning to less experienced white labor. In service trades such as barbering, traditionally a black enclave, new laws prohibiting physical contact between the races handed white customers over to new white businesses at the expense of successful black ones. Those blacks already in the industrial economy were summarily demoted from skilled positions to the lowest, menial trades, even as Washington and his white supporters preached of the need for Negroes to better themselves. Unionism, rather than uniting the common interests of the black and white working classes, provided a way for whites to break into and then commandeer black trades, forever damaging the reputation of organized labor in the black community. At the polling place, higher and higher hurdles were placed before black voters, all but disfranchising them.

Jim Crow laws weren't restricted to the workplace; the entire fabric of social life was restructured in the 1890s to accommodate New South racism. In Atlanta, a city supposedly too busy making money to worry about race, parks that African Americans had once wandered through, including Grant Park Zoo where they'd taken their children, were now off limits to them or divided into sections, the "colored" usually without the benches and fountains of the "white." The city's streetcars were segregated in 1900, and though black Atlanta boycotted them for a time, the system's large white ridership rendered this early attempt at mass protest ineffective. Stores established separate entrances, built separate counters. Even supposedly enlightened institutions such as the Carnegie Library now closed their doors to a black face. In courtrooms, bailiffs placed a "colored" Bible next to the "white" one. Black citizens of the South were reduced to a shadow class.

Segregation was not inevitable. It was not the transition between slavery and the modern civil rights era. Long before the likes of Martin Luther King and Malcolm X, an earlier generation of black men and women had seen the Promised Land of full participation in American life, and then had been forcibly removed from it. Segregation meant hope stolen, clocks turned back, waking up to find you were still in the nightmare. Although he often operated behind the scenes to blunt the effects of segregation, for example, secretly funding court challenges, Booker T. Washington also used segregation to build a power base. With his unique access to white America, he became boss of a patronage system doling out jobs and recommendations to African Americans who toed the Tuskegee line, spying on and discrediting those who did not. That functional black business and academic communities developed in Atlanta at the turn of the century says little about the supposed racial openness of New South Atlanta or black "progress," and volumes about the ability of the city's black community to make a meal out of crumbs.

Less than two miles southwest of Piedmont Park, as Washington waved his white flag, a two-year-old boy named Walter Francis White toddled through his family's prim, well-kept house at 129 Houston Street. Nearly sixty years later this same boy would edge Thurgood Marshall away from the mircophone outside the Supreme Court Building in Washington, D.C., to announce that *Brown v. Board of Education* had put an end to federally sanctioned segregation, a moment he had no small role in creating. Until his death on March 21, 1955, Walter White devoted himself to

a day-to-day repudiation of Booker T. Washington's Atlanta
Compromise and the end of "separate but equal."

*

At this point just about every writer who addresses White's
life qualifies his existence with a sentence along the lines of
"Although he was blond and blue–eyed with fair skin, White
was legally black." Rather than the aberrant being he's usually portrayed as—a freak of nature who somehow used
his fair skin to deceive both white and black America—it's
more accurate to say that White was blond, blue-eyed, fair-
skinned, *and* black. Among the upper reaches of Atlanta's
black community where White was born and raised, fair-
skinned and black were not mutually exclusive concepts.

And though fair skin conferred benefits both during and
after slavery, becoming in many places the determining factor in an unofficial caste system, it didn't enter black families by choice. This was true with the White family as much
as any other. Dilsia, White's great grandmother, produced
six children in the 1830s by her owner, the future president
William Henry Harrison. When Harrison decided to run for
the White House, he handed four of his slave children to his
brother, who in turn sold them out of Virginia to a Georgia
man named Poythress. During the years before the war, one
of the four, Marie, White's grandmother, became the concu-
bine of a white doctor named Augustus Ware. Ware eventually started his own (white) family, all the while keeping
Marie conveniently in the house next door where she could
do his laundry and bear him four children. One of the girls,
Madeline, born in 1863 as the product of two presumably
coerced relations, would be Walter White's mother.

One of the advantages of fair skin became apparent as
the four children grew up. Although many affluent Southerners denied the children they forced upon black women,

some did provide for them, often giving these mixed-race African Americans the dubious consolation of an economic leg up over those whose families had escaped the lecheries of slaveowners. Invested into businesses and education, that money then increased and expanded the advantage into the next generation. In time this led to the creation of a fair-skinned upper tier in many black communities. As blood-lines thinned and skin tones grew lighter, some blacks chose to pass as white, while those who chose not to, so-called "voluntary negroes," were often among the most resolute advocates of black rights. Whether out of a genuine affection or a sense of guilt, until his death in 1872 Augustus Ware gave enough to Marie and his four children for Madeline's brother Nathaniel to become a major property owner around their hometown of La Grange, Georgia, and for Madeline in 1879 to attend Clark University in Atlanta, stepping-stones to a better life for both of them.

At Clark, Madeline moved another step up by marrying Marshall King, a wealthy son of a Reconstruction politician, who died after only a year. It's likely that by then she'd also met George White, a man from more simple stock attending Atlanta University. When both of White's parents died within the same year, he could no longer pay for school and had to leave the university; Madeline finished her schooling and became a teacher. Sometime after King's death, George and Madeline became a couple. George, by now a postal worker, had put down a five-hundred-dollar deposit on a lot on Houston Street, and after the two married in 1882 they moved into a rental property and continued saving. Their first three children, George, Alice, and Olive, were born at the rental, but in 1892 George Sr. finally completed a small house on Houston Street where Walter was born on July 1, 1893. Soon this "cottage," as Walter would later call it, was relocated to the rear of the lot so that the industrious George

Sr. could build the handsome two-flat that would become
the ultimate White family homestead.

During the ten years between their marriage and the
birth of their second son, the Whites firmly established
themselves in the highest level of Atlanta's black community. While the next decades would see some black Atlan-
tans accumulate fortunes, George White's solid, if not lucrative, government job as a postal worker conferred status on
the family. Both George and Madeline had attended college,
and George, like his wife, was fair skinned, but their social
standing was tied most of all to the First Congregational
Church, down the street from their home. Throughout the
state of Georgia there were some 400,000 black Baptists and
90,000 African Methodist Episcopalians, but the 3,000 or
so Congregationalists counted among First Church's pews
were the power brokers. Among the signs of black status in
Atlanta, membership at First Church trumped them all.

*

From its very beginning, First Church was exceptional. After
the war the American Missionary Association (AMA) had
established the Storrs School to provide services to freedmen, some of whom joined the Congregationalist faith and
worked with the AMA to found First Church in 1867. An
unusual blend of ex-slaves and white, starch-collared Connecticut missionaries whose religion traced its roots to the
Pilgrims themselves, the congregation worshiped out of
Storrs School until it secured its own building in 1877. By
1882 Atlanta University, which the AMA had started on the
same site soon after the war, had moved to its next location
on Diamond Hill, and under pressure from the advancing
Black Codes, First Church became predominantly black.
While it had always been known for its social services, the
arrival of Reverend Henry H. Proctor in 1894 made First

Church the most active social force in black Atlanta by offering services not just to its congregation but to the entire
community. A classmate of W. E. B. Du Bois's at Fisk University and a graduate of Yale Divinity School, Proctor was
the first African-American pastor of the church. With time
spent up north in New Haven and regular contact with the
AMA and the integrated staff of Atlanta University, Proctor saw himself as a go-between the races and was widely
respected for it. Booker T. Washington, Theodore Roosevelt,
and William Howard Taft all paid him visits.

On Diamond Hill, by the campus of Atlanta University,
lived two other men of genius and hard work who made the
city a capital of black achievement during the early years
of the Jim Crow era. The first was a businessman, Alonzo
Herndon. Born a slave in 1858 and denied by his white father, the light-complected Herndon came to Atlanta in 1883
and within six months was a partner in a Marietta Street
barbershop. Three years later he opened his own shop, re-
bounding from two unfortunate fires until his third, at 66
Peachtree Street, became arguably the nation's most famous
and most luxurious tonsorial parlor and allowed him to open
two more locations in the city. In 1893 he married Adrienne
McNeil, an actress and drama teacher of unusual refinement
from Savannah, after months of courtship during which she
boarded with the Whites on Houston Street. The 1900 law
forbidding his black barbers from serving white clients didn't
financially devastate Herndon—he was already wealthy by
then from his shrewd real estate investments—but it did
limit his ambitions in personal service. So he redirected his
money into the insurance business and in 1905 founded the
company that would become Atlanta Life. By his death in
1927, Herndon was the richest black man in Atlanta.

Although poorly educated, Herndon was a man of great
natural charm and intellect. Elegant Adrienne, one of the

first black members of Atlanta University's faculty, filed down his rough edges, and together they established themselves as the first family of black Atlanta, admired for their wealth but beloved for their culture and philanthropy. By seeding social projects and business ventures throughout the Atlanta area, Herndon inspired a generation of civic-minded black businessmen, managing, like all great salesmen, to be all things to all people. While a prime example of Tuskegee principles—self-made, all about effort and business savvy—he diplomatically straddled the tricky line between Washington's compromise and Du Bois's demands for full black participation by also supporting the liberal arts at Atlanta University and Du Bois's emergent movement for civil rights. Above all else, Herndon was a pragmatist, never identifying too much with one side or the other, working behind the scenes and footing bills without making pronouncements that might endanger his business interests or standing. As perhaps the best salesman in a city filled with salesmen, he won the respect—if not the equality—of white, boomtown Atlanta. White says nothing about Herndon in his autobiography, but Herndon's pragmatism infuses his career.

Herndon's neighbor near Atlanta University was one of the nation's great thinkers, a man whose philosophy still illuminates African-American life. When W. E. B. Du Bois moved to Atlanta in 1898, having just finished his landmark sociological study *The Philadelphia Negro*, he immediately turned the city with its concentration of five black colleges into one of America's intellectual capitals, even if the city's white leaders had no clue of it. During the next twelve years, until he accepted the job as director of publicity and research of the NAACP in New York, Du Bois set in motion pioneering investigations into black life in America, wrote *The Souls of Black Folk*, and launched the attack on Booker T. Washington that effectively ended Tuskegee's grip on the direction of black America, reawakening the cause of civil rights with a genius met in equal parts by his passion and his intimidating presence. Educated at Harvard and the University of Berlin, forbidding and foppish, Du Bois seemed to tower over his surroundings even though he was only medium height on a good day. By the time Walter White enrolled in Atlanta University, Du Bois had taken his spats and cane north, but his influence on Diamond Hill and within the White family was still strong; Du Bois had known Walter's parents and had taught two of the older White children in college. In the end, White and Du Bois would be enemies, with history offering a better place to the elder, but even if they refused to acknowledge it, their shared vision would always be greater than their differences.

By confronting segregation and the challenges of African-American life with a broad range of weapons, Proctor, Herndon, and Du Bois united the entire spectrum of black Atlanta. Unlike many other Southern cities where those of mixed race tried to huddle in their own, third-racial caste, the more cooperative ethic of Atlanta spawned academic and business leaders who relied on men and women of all shades for success. This isn't to say that skin color didn't matter; there was a reason that the overwhelming proportion of fair-skinned blacks belonged to First Church, including Herndon, who was treasurer. But what differences existed—and they *did* exist—were usually kept in the family. By its own efforts, not the largesse of white Atlanta, the city's black community offered a hopeful place for African Americans at the turn of the century.

*

In the shadow of Proctor's First Church (literally so once the second church building was completed in 1908), the blocky tower reminding him of his duty to his fellow man, be he white or—especially—black, Walter White grew up in a circle that honored practical, financial success in the form of Herndon as much as it did philosophy, art, and the question of rights as proposed by Du Bois.

Certainly First Congregational Church and its commitment to service had a direct and intense impact on the White household. How better to claim a place in America than by worshiping the same faith as its Pilgrim fathers? Not only was George White a deacon at the church, but Reverend Proctor became a family friend. Along with a third family— the Ruckers—the Proctors and the Whites quickly formed their own informal set within the community. One of the few childhood photos of Walter shows him in a crew cut and short pants, pointing at the word "squirrel" neatly scribed on a school chalkboard as Lucy Rucker sits in her pinafore nearby. Each of Walter's three younger sisters, Ruby, Helen, and Madeline, was also matched with a Rucker and a Proctor child the same age. Later, Walter's older brother George would become principal of an American Missionary Association school in Alabama.

Given the depth of his commitment to First Church, it's hard to picture George White building his home down the street as a coincidence. Inside and out, the White house was all things George wanted to be: clean, respectable, orderly, and close to the church. For Madeline, a member of the Twelve Club, the pinnacle of black society in Atlanta, whose doilies and bell jars would not have been out of place in Boston or Hartford, the fresh paint and manicured lawn may have spoken of more earthly desires.

With their children, George and Madeline took the kind but firm approach favored by a religion born out of rocky New England soil. Hard work, regular schedules, and the example of their parents instilled discipline and drive in the

George White, Walter White's father. Quiet, firm, and much beloved by his family, the painful circumstances around his accidental death were compounded by confusion in the hospital regarding his race. *(Yale Collection of American Literature, Beinecke Rare Book and Manuscript Library)*

Madeline White, matriarch of the White family. Her strong personality helped form her son's moral ambitions as well as his personal pretensions. *(Yale Collection of American Literature, Beinecke Rare Book and Manuscript Library)*

White children. Madeline, a thick, imposing woman with strong opinions, assigned duties to every day of the week, with Saturdays the busiest, filled with preparations for the Sabbath. George, by all accounts a gentle, soft-spoken teetotaler, ran his house with pious authority, a Southern black man who lived and worshiped like a Victorian Yankee—cool, rational, and thoroughly unemotional in his dealings with the divine. In his autobiography, *A Man Called White*, Walter describes in great detail the regular ordeal of Sundays under his father's regime: stuffy, interminable hours spent on horsehair kneelers or locked in his room in silent meditation so boring that he all but begged to do homework. Since George forbid all novels less than twenty-five years old, out of desperation Walter had read Dickens, Thackeray, and Trollope by the time he was twelve.

Blond and blue-eyed like his mother, full of energy and humor, young Walter was doted on by his family, maybe even spoiled, but he was hardly a Milquetoast. When he was eight, he threw a rock at a white child who called him a "nigger" for drinking out of a restricted fountain. Already displaying skills of deception that would later serve him well as an investigator (and poorly as a manager), he would order his younger sisters to haul coal for him instead of doing it himself. Still, George White's boy was not afraid of work. By ten, if he couldn't be found at Gate City Colored Public School, he was running errands for I. Kalish, a white tailor on Peachtree Street, or hauling his father's government cart, helping him pick up the afternoon mail. As a teenager he relied on First Church for much of his social life, going to the Sunday afternoon youth service and participating in the Christian Endeavor program with his sisters. The worst punishment his father ever had to mete out to him was a whipping when Walter was in college and was caught smoking one day on his way home from his shift as a page at the Piedmont Hotel. (As an adult, White would chain-smoke and down vast amounts of scotch.) Skinny, jumpy, always ready with a joke or comment, White never stopped moving. Great things were expected of him, and he surely expected them for himself.

*

The most important moment in White's early life took place in September 1906, during the tragic Atlanta Race Riot, and it goes directly to the question of where, exactly, the White family, and in particular Walter, placed themselves within black Atlanta. While there's no question that Madeline and George White saw themselves as black, and taught their children to identify themselves the same way, there's a difference between knowing something and feeling something.

Walter *knew* he was black; he recounts fights between gangs of white and black children in which he proudly took part, defending the turf around First Church. The rock-throwing incident when he's eight shows a pride and sense of self-preservation that serves him well later in his life. But it's not clear that he *felt* black as a child, or at least didn't believe himself subject to all it entailed in turn-of-the-century Atlanta. His mother's reaction—she laughed, fended off the furious white mother knocking on her door, and then gave Walter a perfunctory switching—in no way resembles the life-or-death warning a darker, or less socially secure, black parent would probably have given her child at that time and in that place.

Walter's later writings show that he was well aware of the conflicts between class and caste behind the black community's unified front. In his novel *Flight*, the mixed-race Mimi Daquin comes to Atlanta and notices unspoken divisions: "She in the few days she had been in Atlanta had heard enough to know there were churches attended in the main only by coloured people who were mulattoes or quadroons, others only by those whose complexions were quite dark. . . . All too frequently opportunity came in a direct ratio to the absence of pigmentation."

The White family availed themselves of these kinds of opportunities. Downtown, Madeline and some of the other fair-skinned families could shop with white-level service at the major department stores, though they sometimes encountered problems on the city's segregated streetcars. When they sat in back with the blacks, the whites up front, assuming they were also Caucasian, would insult them for showing solidarity; but if they sat up front, the blacks who knew them would accuse them of trying to pass. George solved the problem by purchasing a surrey for their personal use, yet what stands out is the fact that many blacks in their

circle had long before sworn off the use of segregated streetcars after the boycott of 1900 failed. In college Walter unknowingly took a "white" job as a page at the Piedmont, but
when he discovered the situation he didn't quit in protest.
As politically involved and committed as they were, if they
weren't asked what their race was, the Whites did not feel it
their responsibility to offer the information. Solidarity had
it limits.

As sins go, these are fairly venial, and the Whites were
surely not the only fair-skinned family to commit them.
Obviously they were aware that First Church was a predominantly fair-skinned congregation, and they accepted
Reverend Proctor's sense of noblesse oblige as the price and
responsibility of their position. It's even possible that, given
Proctor's belief in his mediator position between the races,
the Whites viewed these kinds of acts as a positive good, a
sign to both sides that interaction must take place whenever
and however it could, even if that included being allowing to
try on clothes at a department store. Such a mind-set would
be totally consistent with Walter's behavior as an adult.

Walter not only saw the advantages of his light skin; he
was also sensitive at a young age to antagonism it caused.
In a 1947 essay for the *Saturday Review*, White wrote, "The
Negroes resented our white skin, and the ethical standards
which my parents maintained themselves and required of
their children." Later that year, in his newly published autobiography, White admires his parents for guiding "themselves and us along the course between the Scylla of white
hostility and the Charybdis of some Negroes' resentment
against us because we occupied a slightly more comfortable
and better-kept home and were less dark than they."

Although their house was hardly the only reason for the
resentment, the two-flat at 129 Houston declared what and
who the Whites considered themselves. Their neighbor-

hood, a few integrated blocks between the white working-class fringes of Five Points and the far edge of the Fourth Ward, was by no means a ghetto, but Walter describes it as "deteriorating," and the house as the object of envy from slovenly whites and, implicitly, derision from blacks who sensed airs in George's program of constant maintenance and improvement. Understandably the White family had an attitude about a place George had worked for, saved for, and built. Their pride in their home, excessive as it may have been, spoke of their self-worth and expectations. The house, then, broadcasting George's message of right living and fealty to First Church, stood not just on the border of white and black; it also crossed borders within blackness. Living in it required a constant calculus to know who you were. But what nearly happened to it in the bloody September of 1906 taught Walter White to finally *feel* once and for all that he was black.

Through that summer, Hoke Smith, a reforming populist, ran against Clark Howell, publisher of the *Atlanta Constitution*, for the Democratic gubernatorial nomination, which would, considering Georgia's disdain for the Republican party, sew up the general election. While Smith ran initially on a broader platform, Howell went immediately to race and accused Smith of being less than hard line in his hatred of African Americans. Smith reached out to Tom Watson, the Populist politician who had become rabidly anti-black after the Democrats had rolled over his party in 1896. He sought to heal the rift between them by calling for the disfranchisement of blacks. From that point on, the primary race became a contest of racist bile, a dubious exercise in democracy that left Smith the winner and Atlanta's newspapers wanting more. With the political race-baiting ended, the publishers now sold papers with false headlines about black men assaulting white women. By September 22 the city was dry

tinder. That afternoon the *Evening News* sent out a series
of extras, each new one alleging yet another fresh assault on
a white woman. White Atlanta whipped itself into a panic,
mobs formed on street corners, and when night fell, three
days of deadly violence began that would leave twenty-five
blacks dead, hundreds injured, and whatever remained of
Washington's 1895 compromise in tatters.

White described the riot several times over the years,
first in his novel *Flight* and then most completely twenty
years later in his autobiography in a chapter called "I Learn
What I Am." *Flight*, written in 1927, is White's second, less
successful novel, and the riot scene is shown through the
eyes of its mixed-race heroine Mimi. Given that White later
admitted that Mimi shared much in common with him,
she can be fairly mined for his thoughts and impressions.
"I Learn What I Am" from 1947 is, on the other hand, after
two novels, a stab at a third, and countless bits of stage and
screenwriting, arguably the strongest nine pages White ever
wrote and the subject of some controversy.

Although it's only in *Flight* where he describes the city
in an arresting, if sophomoric, image as "a huge boil, packed
tight with putrescence," certain details appear in both pieces.
In *A Man Called White*, he's out collecting the mail with his
father when they hear the roar of a crowd. Coming down the
main business avenue of the city, Peachtree Street, the two
see a lame bootblack from Herndon's barbershop beaten to
death by a white mob. Mimi Daquin takes a slightly different path, arriving at Five Points before Peachtree Street, but
sees the same murder. Skin coloring plays a role in both, too.
Fair skin lets White and his father move through the mobs
without attack, while in *Flight*, Mimi and her father Jean
are confronted by a mob but allowed to pass once the thugs
have a closer look at them. The final image White portrays
in both is a wagon with a few blacks hanging on for their

lives as the white driver alternately whips the horses on and fends off white attackers.

Flight drops off after this first night of terror, but the first chapter of *A Man Called White* goes further. The next evening, after a day of silent expectation, darkness falls and the White family huddle in their home, having heard rumors of a mob coming to "clean out the niggers" on the fringes of the Fourth Ward. According to White, Madeline urges George to get a gun. Around midnight they hear the mob in the distance. George hustles his wife and daughters into the back of the house, then he hands the gun to Walter and says, "Son, don't shoot until the first man puts his foot on the lawn and then—don't you miss!" At that moment, whatever he may have *known* before—his family's principled blackness, the advantages conferred by their light skin that even the night before had saved his life—as White stared into the dark, waiting to defend his family and their totemic home against an unthinking, bloodthirsty white mob, he realized that he was black. Walter White finally *felt* black.

"I Learn What I Am" is a tremendous bit of agitprop, crafted to achieve maximum dramatic effect. The question, for White's prime biographer Kenneth Janken, is whether there really was a gun in the White house that night. In a letter to his literary agent from the year of *Flight*'s publication, White talks about the riot without ever mentioning a gun, but then, in a magazine profile of him in *The Nation* from 1930 and in an unpublished article from 1934, the gun suddenly appears. Surely such an important, dramatic detail would have figured in any telling of the story. More damning are the bemused reactions of his sisters Alice and Madeline to his later recollections, wondering themselves where the gun came from.

Did White fudge this detail? Probably. *Flight* was unabashed political literature, and by the time the gun appeared in 1930, White's books and articles had helped make him famous. If he took a literary license, it's most likely he did so knowing that the possibility of this young man being forced into violence by his white neighbors heightened the stakes and made the story better. In our time, when the purity of raw facts is made to compensate for the general unreality of the age, this fiddling with the details may raise ethical concerns, but storytelling of a sort White surely grew up with in the Fourth Ward played a major role in his elevation to power in the 1920s. As later chapters will show, fact-checking mattered less to White than making his greater point, advancing the cause, and making himself look good. The means, to him, were not as important as the end, and that extended to the written word.

But as usual with White, there's another layer. Janken believes that White, insecure in his racial identity, inserted the gun in the story to establish his credibility as African American at a moment when W. E. B. Du Bois was questioning his blackness. Thirty years earlier, John Hope, president of Morehouse College, another member of Atlanta's light-skinned elite, with ties to George White's family back in Augusta, had had a similar brush with mob violence as a boy in Hamburg, South Carolina. The experience was not easily forgotten. According to *The Story of John Hope*, "In discussions of race prejudice, John Hope would often add, 'And remember, I heard the guns of the Hamburg Massacre.'" To have your sense of racial identity forged in battle made for powerful stuff, and it certainly trumped Du Bois's own tale of racial awakening, which involved a little white girl in Great Barrington, Massachusetts, rejecting the visiting card of ten-year-old Willie Du Bois. During the riot, Du Bois had sat in front of his house with a rifle in his lap; John Hope did the same at Morehouse. White could very well have wanted to have a gun too.

Yet while credibility later became a concern for White during Du Bois's attacks and the hardships of the depression, insecurity was not. If he was so desperate to prove he was black, it's remarkable that in "I Learn What I Am" he refuses to tiptoe with terms like "fair" and "light," and a number of times simply refers to his skin as "white." He may well have thought he was a "better" sort of black, but White never doubted he was black himself. More often, White didn't do *enough* to establish his credibility with black America, assuming too often that they knew and believed he was working for all their interests and not just his own. Any discussion of White's credibility or identity or blackness, though, dissolves without a definition of what, exactly, makes a person black in America. Is it blood? If so, how much? One drop? The 5/32nds of Walter White that made him "legally" black in 1906 Atlanta? Or is it, instead, cultural, or economic?

The obvious and assumed, the supposed common sense of Du Bois's Jim-Crow-in-Georgia rule, have too many exceptions like the White family to hold the answer. We will never define "blackness" in a way acceptable to all, but during that night in 1906 White created his own definition of what black is:

"Theirs [the whites] was a world of contrasts in values: superior and inferior, profit and loss, cooperative and noncooperative, civilized and aboriginal, white and black. If you were on the wrong end of the comparison, . . . then you were marked for excision, expulsion, or extinction. I was a Negro; I was therefore that part of history which opposed the good, the just, and the enlightened. I was a Persian, falling before the hordes of Alexander. I was a Carthaginian, extinguished by the Legions of Rome. . . . I was the defeated, wherever and whenever there was a defeat."

Yes, blood mattered, he decided, but to White blackness meant living within the subtleties, in active opposition to the simple, arbitrary differences enforced by the European impulse to conquer and classify. Instead of finding a place for himself on the fringes of his race, White made himself its center, the very definition of what black is. As Du Bois would later put it, "He seemed really to believe that his personal interests and the interest of his race and organization were identical." A few lines later in his autobiography, White admits that his white skin over a black soul is "inexplicable," but instead of the insecurity Janken stresses, he boasts of the heroism of the situation with a self-congratulating idealism that's admirable all the same. Whether the gun existed or not doesn't matter as much as the truth that followed—White never identified himself as Caucasian. He left that to others, from Tennessee crackers to Clarence Darrow and H. G. Wells. If he ever passed as white, it was as a play against whites. He always felt black because, in the most primal sort of identity politics, he had defined blackness as the way *he* saw the world.

The White home was not burned that night. Shots from another group of blacks put out the streetlight, scaring away the white mob. As keeper of this house that physically embodied an idea Du Bois did not create but merely identified as the Talented Tenth—the exceptional cutting edge of a people on the way up—Walter had found his place within society: in a house between two worlds, but one that was really a world of its own.

CHAPTER TWO

The Life Insurance Temperament

~ Since Atlanta did not provide public high schools for the city's black children, Walter enrolled in Atlanta University's prep program in 1908 and delivered grades that must have raised George and Madeline's eyebrows: mediocre Cs, with truly awful scores in vocational subjects balanced out by As and Bs in some of the humanities. For all the high hopes attached to him, Walter was no scholar; luckily history doesn't require a transcript. White's gifts—a sharp wit, a commanding attitude, and an apparently bottomless well of energy—were great tools outside the classroom, and he continued to make use of them working summer jobs. As high school came to a close, Walter pulled himself together enough to get into Atlanta University in the fall of 1912.

Of the five black colleges in Atlanta—AU, all-men's Morehouse, all-women's Spelman, Clark, and Morris Brown—AU was the most prestigious, its seven buildings on Diamond Hill covered with ivy as thick as any on the halls of Yale. The resemblance was no accident. After the Civil War the same AMA missionaries that had founded First Congregational Church had plucked methods, mission, and even teachers out of New Haven, then dropped them onto these sixty acres of bare hill overlooking downtown Atlanta to create Atlanta University. Tended with a beneficent repression that would

Walter graduated from the Atlanta University
prep program in 1912 with an unexceptional
record, just good enough to get him into Atlanta University. *(Library of Congress)*

have been very familiar to Walter, the students were taught
the ways of New England Brahminhood through a rigorous
liberal arts curriculum.

From the moment he walked onto the campus, White
threw his bounding enthusiasm into clubs and teams. During his four years at AU he was assistant manager and occasional contributor to *The Scroll*, the monthly student paper;
a varsity debater; an actor in *The Taming of the Shrew*; and,
most of all, an athlete. Nicknamed "Fuzzy" for his thin,
flyaway hair, he glowers from team photos of the Crimson
and Gray football squad taken in front of Stone Hall, first
to the eye for his white skin. Playing schools such as Morris Brown, Clark, and Macon's Haines Institute, the team

went 1-2-1 in 1912. White was on the small side, but so was AU, so he usually made the squad, even playing quarterback his senior year. In the spring he patrolled centerfield for the baseball team and, as he showed in his aborted novel *Blackjack*, had a taste for boxing too.

Not all his distractions were of the character-building sort. As he admits in his autobiography, many fellow students thought Walter "too young and too much interested in having a good time to do a responsible job satisfactorily." A jot in *The Scroll* from 1913 evidences some romantic intrigues: "Mr. W.F.W. has a fondness for singing 'You'll never know the good fellow I am till I've gone away.' Strange to say Miss C. W. constantly sings 'I want you back.'" He was, of course, a frat boy too, pledging with the Owls, yet another exclusive group within the group, and yet again he reports he was "resented" for his "color and financial status." Even so, his classmates saw a leader in this high-strung, brash young man, and elected him president of the Class of 1916.

The school had other lessons for Walter White beyond those of a liberal arts education. AU's faculty drew not only from white New England but also included over the years outstanding black scholars. With the horrors of the 1906 riot fresh in his mind and a rising tide of racial violence around the nation that could only be called a mania—in 1916, for example, a mob in Kingsport, Tennessee, used a crane to *lynch* a rogue elephant—the interaction between sincere, intelligent, and open-minded educators of both races proved the value of integration to Walter. "It was they," wrote White, "who saved me from the defeatist belief that all whites are evil and bigoted . . ." Infused with an abolition spirit, the school made no secret of its strong advocacy of civil rights. In Walter's freshman year, Arthur Spingarn, then on the board of the fledgling NAACP, spoke in the chapel the Monday morning before Christmas. It's easy to imagine White there, singing

"Do You Think I'll Make a Soldier?" along with the rest of the student body.

During the summers he worked, as much to be in the world as to bring in some money to a household already stretched on George's postal salary. If Walter's financial status was in any way exalted, it was only relative to his fellow students. The page job at the Piedmont Hotel came between freshman and sophomore years, and it was Fred Toomer, ahead of him at AU and the hotel's bell captain, who convinced him to stay. When offered an even better job the next summer, though, White fessed up and took a job as a bellhop at another hotel, down a few stars from the Piedmont, where he got a less genteel view of white society. As the end of his junior year approached, he resolved that his days of toting suitcases were over.

*

If September 1906 had ended Walter's childhood, the summer of 1915 turned him into a man. Rather than stay close to home, he became a traveling salesman for a local black-owned insurance firm, Standard Life. Between Atlanta Mutual (Herndon's company), Standard, and a handful of other concerns, the city proper had been played out for prospects, so White went into the countryside, walking the small towns around Atlanta, earning only what commissions brought him. It was not easy work for black agents. In these early days of black entrepreneurship, many black customers doubted the resources and reliability of black-owned companies despite the strong element of racial uplift underpinning insurance at the time. It could also be dangerous work. Aside from having to travel Jim Crow, black men in suits with briefcases in hand, trying to do business, attracted unwanted attention from whites who in some towns outlawed them altogether. Walter's light skin let him move through the outskirts of Atlanta untroubled, at least on the surface. Keeping to the "If Not Asked, Don't Tell" policy of the White family, Walter was able to talk to both country blacks and poor whites who would just as soon have shot him if they'd known his true identity.

One topic was certainly the lynching of Leo Frank. A New Yorker and a Jew, Frank had been accused of the rape and murder of young Mary Fagan, a girl employed at the Atlanta pencil factory he ran. His trial in 1913 was a sham, the courtroom filled with armed men and the jury under threat to find him guilty, which they quickly did. Once again Tom Watson fanned the hatred. Although the governor of Georgia, John Slaton, commuted Frank's sentence to life in prison, that wasn't enough for Watson and much of white Georgia—in 1915 Frank was hauled out of his cell and lynched. Watson, on the other hand, was elected that fall to the U.S. Senate.

Another volatile topic was D. W. Griffith's film *The Birth of a Nation*. Although few rural Georgians had ever seen a motion picture in 1915, let alone this one, the controversy and hatred it stirred up after its spring premieres in Los Angeles and New York served notice that the new medium of cinema would have an enormous impact on the culture. Based on Thomas Dixon's racist novel *The Clansman*, *The Birth of a Nation* on one hand created the grammar of film and at the same time incited not only specific acts of violence against blacks—"That show certainly does make you hate those blacks," said one viewer in New York—but also helped reignite interest in the Ku Klux Klan. To counter the film and its effects, the NAACP stepped into the fight and for the first time made itself known nationally through its organized protests.

White didn't make a whole lot of money that summer—selling industrial insurance door-to-door was not the work of rich men—but the three themes that would dominate his life had come forward all at once: lynching, the power of media, and the NAACP. That fall he returned to AU a driven man. He kept on with Standard, preparing actuarial tables for them in his spare time; he debated, and of course he was quarterback for the Crimson and Gray. But after his months on the road, a black man weaving secretly through the coarse fabric of white Georgia and coming out alive; a summer spent listening to an untold number of his fellow Americans applauding a dangerously effective work of art and the lynching of an innocent man—Walter began the school year with a letter to W. E. B. Du Bois at the NAACP in New York, asking directions for establishing a branch chapter at AU. Du Bois passed the letter on to the secretary, May Childs Nerney. After a rather dissuasive response from Miss Nerney, the idea seems to float away. But the eager college senior, through the offices of his future nemesis Du Bois, had announced his presence to 70 Fifth Avenue.

*

Commencement for the Atlanta University Class of 1916 took place on Wednesday, May 31, of that year. Selections by Dvořák and Mendelssohn were sung by the school chorus, an address given by Reverend C. Breckinridge Wilmer, and an oration entitled "The Economic and Political Future of the American Negro" delivered by Walter Francis White. Mae Belle Maxwell of Decatur received the highest academic honors among the seven graduates, but Walter had his own distinction in the class as the only one of them not intent on becoming a teacher. He could've been a principal at an AMA school in Albany, a sojourn not unlike Du Bois's two summers teaching in a school in backwoods Tennessee, or his brother George's life in Alabama, but Walter White wasn't made for teaching.

What *would* he do? "Education and work," wrote Du Bois in his 1903 essay "The Talented Tenth," "are the levers to uplift a people. Work alone will not do it unless inspired by the right ideals and guided by intelligence. . . . The Negro race, like all other races, is going to be saved by its exceptional men." Well, White had the liberal education; he'd been guided all his twenty-two years by right ideals; he had intelligence, if not Du Bois's titanic mind; and he knew how to put in a day's work. More than anything else, though, from head to toe, inside and out, Walter White *was* exceptional. By fate and by design, he was like no one else, a permanent minority wherever he went.

The question remained, how would White do his leading? According to his sister Madeline, he wanted to become a lawyer, but their parents "were not able to send him to a law school that he wished to go to." White never mentions becoming a lawyer in his autobiography, a curious omission. Since he was known throughout college as a partier, it's possible that his grades were the issue, not money. And considering the depth of White's connections throughout black Atlanta, it's hard to believe that if a promising young scholar among them needed help, he wouldn't have gotten it. With law out of the question for whatever reason, White went in a different direction. The day after graduation he started work at the Standard Life Insurance Company.

Insurance, and especially black-owned insurance companies, had a social and economic role in black society that went far beyond paying out claims. W. J. Graham's passionately titled *The Romance of Life Insurance* claimed the prophet Joseph as the world's first insurance man: he advised the Egyptians to store away part of each harvest for the inevitable lean years. As much of a reach as that is, the truth does have its roots in Africa, where burial societies and the mutual care of village life came over with the slaves in the seventeenth century. While obviously the slaves couldn't re-knit the fracture of large-scale, group customs, mutual aid and benevolent societies such as the African Union Society of Newport, Rhode Island, and Philadelphia's Free African Society, created by freedmen in the late eighteenth century, pooled capital to spread individual economic burdens across the group. Along with their contributions, members agreed to subscribe to specific codes of behavior, further strength-ening the foundation of the communities. After the Civil War, mutual-aid societies widened the scope of their bene-fits beyond the issues of church and home to establish small banks and make investments in black-owned businesses. The emergence of industrial insurance, paid for on a weekly or monthly basis, let the poor finally afford insurance with-out having to join a mutual aid society, shifting power away from these unregulated organizations which sometimes found themselves on dodgy financial ground—the collapse of Atlanta's Odd Fellows Lodge in 1916 was a major blow to the Fourth Ward both economically and psychologically—and allowing more stable investment of black capital. By the turn of the century, the first black insurance companies were incorporated.

Opinion of insurance in the black community was still di-vided as Walter made his choice. Atlanta had greeted Alonzo Herndon as a hero when he'd purchased Atlanta Benevolent in 1905, cheering his philanthropy while pretending not to notice the enormous windfall it would bring him in the years to come. But by the teens the financial motivation woven into the business led some of the more theoretical types at AU to turn up their noses at insurance men. Social minis-ters, Reverend Proctor in particular, disdained insurance for the same reasons most ministers were suspicious of lodges, fearing they took influence—and, one supposes, money—away from the churches. Even so, Atlanta University and the city's other black colleges would provide the core leaders of an industry that a 1917 investigation of black progress said demanded "individuals with liberal intellectual culture, efficient business training, and keen business sense."

Surrounded by so many good men with ambitions for both social justice and fat bank accounts, men who felt their value to the race came in action, not in further study, White fit right in. But the match was not purely a matter of racial uplift and financial goals; Walter White, it seemed, was born for insurance. Consider the following list describing "The Life Insurance Temperament," from *Life Insurance as a Life Work* (1926):

1) A desire to sell something
2) Enjoyment in meeting strangers, the social instinct
3) The impulse to give expression to your ideas, and to have others believe as you do
4) Confidence in your ability successfully to accomplish whatever you set out to do
5) Love of the thrill that comes from a hard fight for a good cause
6) Tendency to want to dominate those with whom you come in contact
7) A gift for being tactful
8) The kind of personality that causes people to like you as soon as they meet you, and to continue liking you thereafter
9) The courage of your convictions
10) Initiative—the compelling desire to start something
11) The go getter attitude, with a preference for dealing with people, rather than with papers
12) A boundless energy
13) A desire to serve
14) Vision which enables you to see far into the future

That, in fourteen points, was Walter Francis White.

Other books on the calling that was Insurance demanded clean clothes, crisp collars, and full heels; hands and fingernails were to be well kept. As if following an old salesman's manual, White stayed dapper all his life, indulging in a taste for bespoke suits even on his not-for-profit salary.

If insurance looked to be the perfect field for his talents, Standard Life was the perfect home. Atlanta Life plodded along like Herndon, quietly building up a stockpile of cash, but Standard Life took its cue from its more progressive president, Heman Perry, aggressively pursuing clients and pouring their money back into black businesses with the same passion and creativity. Founded in 1908, by the summer White first wandered those rural towns Standard had almost $2 million of insurance in force and nearly half a million dollars in assets. Many considered it the nation's most successful black-owned business, and by the time of its eventual downfall in 1924, Standard Life had diversified into businesses such as printing, real estate, pharmacies, engineering, and farming through a system of interrelated corporations.

While Harry Pace, a former student and business partner of Du Bois's who would later found Black Swan records, the first black recording company, served as secretary-treasurer, Standard Life took its cues from Perry, described in promotional material as "a combination of sterling integrity, youthful vigor and enthusiasm, forceful personality, broad vision, and unselfish service." A dictator in his own office, Perry expected his employees to give as much as he did to the company, which was everything. He'd sworn off liquor, sworn off tobacco, maybe even sworn off marriage—he was a confirmed bachelor—for his dream, and he didn't allow the ugly facts to get in the way of its success. Once, when an accountant gave him the company's balance sheets, rightly concerned that Standard was spiraling downward, Perry tossed the liabilities page into the garbage and simply read the assets.

Walter White, still living at home, started as a clerk, selling policies during the evenings and on weekends until he was promoted to cashier, a job he modestly described as "less imposing and responsible than it sounds," but which at other insurance concerns was deemed a position of no small importance, overseeing the disbursement of all monies going in and out of the company. He was also a director of Standard Loan and Realty, another company under Perry's Standard umbrella. The men of Standard Life, though, didn't sit on their success, and that included White. Race men, they subscribed to the more practical sense evolving out of Du Bois's rarefied Talented Tenth ideal that advancing in one's work equaled advancing the cause. At the same time, though, silently amassing capital like Herndon wasn't keeping young black men from being lynched—sixty-nine of them in 1915. And making money was no longer enough to qualify you as one of the leaders of black Atlanta.

Walter's chance to join those leaders came in the fall of 1916, when news spread that the Atlanta Board of Education planned to build a new white high school and pay for it by ending public education for black students after the sixth grade. Eighth grade had already been eliminated two years before. A city with five excellent private black colleges, Atlanta offered its black population of 75,000 only 14 grammar schools, 13 of which were decrepit wooden sheds forced to operate in shifts to handle the crowding. After church one Sunday, a group of men, many fresh from another of Proctor's sermons, met at the office of Standard Life to discuss the situation. At the suggestion of Harry Pace, they decided to establish an Atlanta branch of the NAACP. White, who'd already tried once, sent a letter that December to Ms. Nerney's replacement, Roy Nash.

The man who responded, field secretary James Weldon
Johnson, would soon become the greatest influence in Walter White's life. A renaissance man who had written for the
Broadway stage, a novelist, lawyer, and journalist as well
as former ambassador to Venezuela and Nicaragua, Johnson had just come aboard the NAACP in 1916. Right now he
focused on working long distance with this young, fellow
AU graduate to create a strong and stable branch office in
a very important city. Everything came to a head on February 22, 1917. A few days earlier the branch—which included
among its members Reverend A. D. Williams, grandfather
of Dr. Martin Luther King, Jr.—had met and selected an executive committee led by Morehouse president John Hope,
Ben Davis of the now-defunct Odd Fellows Lodge, and Du
Bois's close friend George Towns. An emergency committee
would deal with the schools issue—a committee that did not
count White among its number because he was "too young
and hot-headed." On the morning of the 22nd the branch
learned that the Board of Education had moved up its vote
on the high school measure to that afternoon in hopes of
avoiding a black protest. What little organization the branch
had accomplished allowed them to send a small delegation,
which managed to convince one of the white board members that the plan was unfair to the city's black population.
Miraculously, the board then decided not to go ahead with
the high school, planning instead to float a bond measure
that spring.

White wrote two letters to Johnson that day, one in
the morning to advise him of what the branch had accomplished, and another later to report their success. Although
in later life he was accused by some of being overly friendly
with new acquaintances, the playfulness and bluster that
comes through in White's first letter shows that he walked
in the door with it. Discussing plans for Johnson to appear

The Atlanta Branch of the NAACP, 1917. Walter White sits at the right end of the first row, with his friend Dr. Louis T. Wright at his side. Entrepreneur and friend of Du Bois, Harry Pace, sits at the far left. Dr. John Hope stands, second from right. *(Library of Congress)*

at their first public meeting of the branch, twenty-two-year-old White tells the accomplished leader, more than twice his age, "We plan the biggest meeting of its kind ever held in the South and you will have to do some real speaking that night. So you have fair warning now." Overreaching, he closes, "I would appreciate hearing from you at any time that you may find time to write." But it's a postscript that reveals most. After "Very truly yours" and the loopy, cheerful signature that would remain the same until his death, he added his new title: Secretary Atlanta Branch N.A.A.C.P., and then underneath, "(Sounds big, doesn't it?)". At once he manages to be self-effacing and amusing while drawing attention to his real point: his accomplishment.

As many were in the course of White's career, Johnson was charmed by his new protégé's chumminess, but soon he would see another quality in him that would lead to history. In March, Johnson came to Atlanta to stir up black interest in defeating the bond measure which, the branch had been baldly told by the Board of Education, would direct no monies to black schools. Held in the Odd Fellows Building on Auburn Avenue, the meeting seemed to bring out most of the Fourth Ward. Elegant and eloquent, Johnson commanded the stage with his presence, explaining why African Americans needed to dig deep and pay the discriminatory poll tax levied on them in order to vote down the measure. Unlike Du Bois, famous not just for his mind but for his lack of anything resembling a common touch, Johnson had a regal sort of mellow that let others feel his intelligence rather than having it pressed upon them. His style would find a perfect complement in the man who followed him on stage.

When Johnson called upon him to speak, White was completely unprepared. With policemen stationed around the hall, he stood up and delivered what he called "a rabble-rousing speech" that ended with him quoting Patrick Henry's famous "Give me liberty, or give me death!" The crowd went wild, and something must have clicked in Johnson's head even then. Dedicated, experienced, and well suited as he was to his work at the NAACP, Johnson's political career and his work at the *New York Age* had been largely under the aegis of Booker T. Washington, which made Du Bois, among others on the board, wary of him. Run largely by wealthy white philanthropists quite certain that they knew what was best for the Negro, the NAACP relied on Du Bois for its integrity in the black community. The great philosopher, though, was not a great politician. The organization's house organ, *The Crisis*, became under his hand the touchstone of black thought in the early twentieth century, producing revenue and attention but not necessarily action. Johnson understood the need to blast the NAACP into the front part of

America's mind, and that would mean not just the long so-
nority of Du Bois but someone loud, fast, and full of stacatto
energy like White.

In the meantime President Woodrow Wilson had sent
the first American troops into World War I in April 1917,
and White, never one to shirk an adventure, volunteered for
a planned training camp for black officers. The story as he
tells it in his autobiography is pure "Over There" hokum:
he gives a speech at a patriotic meeting and pops up, first in
line, when the call goes out for volunteers. In fact White had
his insurance career to consider, and that still came first,
ahead of war efforts and civil rights. In a letter to Roy Nash,
dated May 9, he asks for information about the proposed
camp, having heard some scuttlebutt about it from an acquaintance. He's interested but not willing to do anything
rash. "I have my future pretty well mapped out," he writes,
"and I do not intend to run the risk of losing all that I have
attained since leaving school for any uncertainty." White ultimately decided to enlist, but after only a few days he and
two other fair-skinned blacks were thrown out of camp because, according to him, of rumors connecting fair-skinned
blacks with German sabotage efforts in the South.

By the fall of 1917 Johnson had convinced Du Bois that
they needed Walter White in New York. The field secretary
had seen him in action and worked with him, and Du Bois
could call on references from the likes of Harry Pace, George
Towns, and John Hope. While Johnson may well have discussed the idea with Walter's parents after that meeting
in March, he first tested the waters with Walter in a letter
dated October 7. "Have matter under advisement," White
telegraphed Johnson two days later. "You realize my position here and my chances for advancement." What followed
were three months of hemming and hawing that must surely have annoyed Johnson no end.

A photo of the executive committee of the Atlanta branch from that year shows eleven men. Ten of them stare at the camera, patiently putting up with the whole thing. And then there's White, by far the youngest—and lightest—man in the group, sitting in front of John Hope and next to his friend Dr. Louis Wright, eyes boring ahead as if he's trying to stare history in the face. White's future in the insurance business, or whatever else he was led to through Standard's sprawling concerns and his work with the NAACP branch, was shaping up to be lucrative. Less than two years out of college and he was running with the biggest names in black Atlanta; everything was pointing to a comfortable life in the capital of the South. The pay at the NAACP would be less than he was making now, and at the end there was no payday, no investment that blossomed into a fortune. Working side by side with Du Bois and James Weldon Johnson, though, two of the most influential men of his race, would put White in contact with wealthy, powerful, creative people. He would be sacrificing his financial future for the good of the cause, even as enlightened success came to equal uplift. And then there was New York. His mother considered it immoral and dangerous, which could only have made it more alluring to him.

While White fretted, Johnson and Du Bois finally overcame board concerns about his youth and inexperience. The assistant secretary, White's proposed title, would be in charge of the main office when the secretary wasn't there, and liaison with all the growing number of branches, so it was a serious position. On December 15 Johnson made the formal offer. A month later there were still letters back and forth, clarifying numbers and questions until Johnson finally ended his January 15 missive with an exasperated "Will you please let me hear from you at the very earliest convenience?"

In the end, George White and Walter's friend, Dr. Louis T. Wright, pushed Walter into his destiny, each playing to one side of the Talented Tenth argument in his own way. George took his son out in the carriage and laid on a quiet sermon worthy of Reverend Proctor, telling him that God had given him many advantages and it was now time he gave back. Certainly this registered with Walter, but the argument of his contemporary probably had greater pull. Wright warned Walter that if he stayed in Atlanta he'd grow rich and bored.

*

On January 31, 1918, Walter White reported for duty at 70 Fifth Avenue in New York, a small office connected to the office of *The Crisis* next door. James Weldon Johnson had met him at the train and taken him under his wing the moment he arrived, placing him in a Harlem boardinghouse and escorting him the next morning to lower Manhattan. The staff on site was limited. John Shillady, a white social worker from Westchester, New York, was taking over for the army-bound Roy Nash as secretary, though his greatest skills were organizational, not inspirational. Office manager Richetta Randolph was fully devoted to Johnson and generally annoyed by everyone else, while the accountant quietly dealt with business affairs. Acting chairman of the board Mary White Ovington, a secular mother superior in service to good causes, swished between the desks. Raised, like White, in the shadow of a famous clergyman, in her case Henry Ward Beecher, Ovington had gone from Radcliffe to working in settlements in New York, where she developed a devotion to the African-American cause that brought her in contact with both Washington and Du Bois. Although quickly wary of the former, she fell under Du Bois's thrall, and the two became close friends. The only white in the Niagara Movement, his precursor to the NAACP, it was Ovington who, with a group of progressive activists, journalists, and thinkers, had issued the manifesto "The Call" that had led to the formation of the NAACP. She was in many ways the conscience of the organization. Next door Du Bois, stroking his goatee, ruled his own roost at *The Crisis*.

Wood-lined, calm, and intense, the NAACP headquarters was filled with hard thought and philosophical discussions about the direction of things. Action was usually limited to the movement of paper from one basket to another and the typing of memos in quadruplicate.

But White had the "go-getter attitude, with a preference for dealing with people, rather than with papers."

The NAACP was about to change.

Undercover Against Lynching

୬୭ On the morning of February 13, 1918, White and Johnson headed to the office, bundled up against another chilly
day in New York. The winter so far throughout much of the
United States had been dark and cold, and a coal shortage
had forced President Wilson to shut down certain industries
to conserve supplies. In the twelve days White had been up
north, he'd rarely strayed far from Johnson, going to work together, taking lunch with him at the Automat, then stealing
a few minutes at Brentano's where the older man had him on
a crash course in the sort of modern literature not taught at
Atlanta University. The day before had been Lincoln's Birthday, as well as the ninth anniversary of "The Call." But the
paper they shared on the train downtown showed how little
progress had been made since then: In a Tennessee hamlet
halfway between Franklin, the birthplace of the Klan, and
Sewanee, the height of Southern academe, a black farmer
named Jim McIlherron had been burned alive for shooting
two white youths. Few other details were forthcoming.

At the NAACP office the ugly symbolism of a Lincoln's
Birthday lynching made the usual telegrams of protest to
the governor and president feel limp. As John Shillady went
ahead and sent them anyway, suddenly White had an idea.
What if he went to Estill Springs, site of the murder, pretending to be white, and got the details himself?

Johnson and Ovington had reservations, to say the least. Other African Americans had personally investigated lynchings before, Ida Wells-Barnett most notably, but never in this way. A black man caught passing in order to spy on whites would be lynched himself. Period. White knew that as well as anyone, but twenty-four years old, straight out of Georgia, looking, as the poet Langston Hughes would describe him, like a "little Irishman," he kept at it, volunteering for this potentially deadly trip like a cocky new kid trying to prove himself.

Johnson knew this wasn't a game—back in 1901 he'd nearly been lynched himself in Jacksonville, Florida—but he'd brought White to New York for exactly this reason, to stir things up. He was a spark plug, not a sociologist. And even if no one had ever considered this kind of mission before, White *was* without question uniquely qualified for it. Not only was his skin light enough to open doors and, hopefully, mouths, but he'd survived the edgy summer of 1915, learned the ways of sleepy Southern towns. How different would this be, really, from those days? Most of all, though, it was what George and Madeline *hadn't* taught their son that mattered most: Walter White was not intimidated by white America.

There's no record of what White said to convince them, but three days later he was on a train to Chattanooga, armed with the Life Insurance Temperament and a set of credentials from the *New York Evening Post* given to him by the paper's publisher, Oswald Garrison Villard, the grandson of abolitionist William Lloyd Garrison and an often contentious member of the NAACP board. If he were caught out somehow, maybe pretending he was a reporter would help him squirm out of trouble.

The trip was shorter than White claims in his autobiography, where he says he spent "days" in Estill Springs, a place "as remote from the outside world as though it had been in Tibet." In fact, after a night in Chattanooga, eighty miles east of Estill Springs, he arrived in the town early on the 18th, and immediately checked into Goddard's boarding-house across the road from the railroad station. After feigning interest in some cotton land for sale by the landlord, White proceeded to the general store and presented himself as a traveling salesman from the Exelento Medicine Company. The townspeople were suspicious of this new arrival, but White reached back into his salesman's training and, in a word, played them. Instead of asking questions, he acted not just ignorant of the lynching but completely indifferent to it, changing the subject until finally the white folks couldn't hold back their pride any longer and laid out all the ghastly details White had come for without him having to even leave his seat at the potbellied stove. McIlherron, it turned out, had owned a large plot of land envied by whites and blacks alike. He was also famously truculent. The teenage boys, well-known troublemakers, had thrown rocks at him. McIlherron had reacted violently and then tried to escape from the town, accompanied by a local minister. The farmer was caught, tortured, and burned, the minister executed.

As he was busy with this "sleuthing," as White calls it, he had the composure to write a remarkable letter to Shillady from the Goddard House, explaining the whole plan in buoyant terms that make it seem as if he's down there playing a practical joke. It's heroic in its way, the product of someone who's already preparing to dine out on his adventure, and finishes with a request that Shillady tell Johnson that they hadn't "lynched his Corona yet." Still, White knew when to get out; the next morning, already back in Chattanooga, he sent a telegram to the office asking whether he should go on to Fayetteville, Georgia, where another lynching had just

taken place. A few days later he was back in New York, safe
and sound. He never looked back at Atlanta.

*

Within two weeks of finding his desk, White had proven himself invaluable to the NAACP. Through 1927 he would eventually investigate forty-one lynchings, eight race riots, and two
cases of widespread peonage, risking his life repeatedly in the
dank backwaters of Florida, the piney woods of Georgia, and
the cotton fields of Arkansas in search of the truth. He didn't
so much enter the scene that February 1918 as he exploded,
initiating nine years of nonstop work that placed him near
the center of every sphere of black political, social, and artistic life in the 1920s. This experience in turn formed his power
base in the following decades. What he accomplished for the
NAACP in the teens and twenties—investigation, congressio-
nal testimony, lobbying, fund-raising, speeches, writings, and
close management of two landmark legal cases—along with
his literary accomplishments and social connections—made
White in many ways the epitome of the New Negro emergent in post–World War I America, a man no longer willing
passively to accept white oppression or simply beg for help.

But the sum of what White achieved in the nine years
after Estill Springs doesn't fully explain the role he came
to play in the imagination of much of black America that
decade. It wasn't just his willingness to cheat death for the
cause. It was *how* he did it that made him special. Every
chance he had, Walter White got in the face of ignorant
white America. He was a provocateur, dodging in and out of
the clutches of danger, tweaking The Man's nose as he did
it, a trickster as annoying and funny and confounding as any
you'd find in a folktale. And as soon as White stood up in
a church basement or on the stage of an auditorium to tell
his stories, that's what he became, a character in a folktale.

Ultimately it was how he described his exploits that proved how well he knew his people and how much he truly belonged to them, at least in the beginning. In time it would put him at the very center of the Harlem Renaissance.

*

Many factors conspired to make Estill Springs a tipping point on lynching in America. As segregation seeped deeper and deeper into the life of the South, lynching had become both a form of terrorist control of the black population and an entertainment for whites. When news of an impending lynching spread through a region, hundreds, sometimes thousands, children in tow, would pour into a town to watch and participate in the torture and murder. Afterward, body parts would often be taken as souvenirs and photo postcards of the event sold. Until now President Wilson, a Virginian who'd had kind words for a *Birth of a Nation* when it premiered, offered nothing more than the occasional small noise of rebuke about lynching, but his silence was becoming an embarrassment. As American troops fought in Europe, there in part because of tales of German atrocities, photos of charred black bodies, mutilated by their fellow countrymen, appeared on the front pages of newspapers at home, shaming more and more Americans. In the South the moneyed interests had noticed that after lynchings, sometimes the black populations of towns or regions left en masse for Detroit, Chicago, or New York, throwing local labor markets into chaos. An end to lynching for the bosses would mean a slowing of the Great Migration north and a return to cheap labor, both black and white.

In the past the NAACP had been content to register protest, but White's derring-do in Tennessee was more than fact-gathering; it was a form of resistance, and it energized the operation to keep the pressure on. Shillady engaged federal and

state officials in a battle of accusations and denials as newspapers, mainly in the North but increasingly in the South,
ran editorials condemning lynching. Two weeks after Estill
Springs, just when the horror of lynching was about to recede
in white American minds, three black men were lynched in
Delhi, Louisiana, followed by another in Monroe, Louisiana,
in mid-March. The trickle of anti-lynching editorials now
became a flow, and even the Kentucky House of Representatives voted 70 to 0 for a constitutional amendment to punish
public servants who allowed lynchings to occur.

The lynchings continued: sixty for all of 1918, escalating
not just in number but in their perverse brutality. After fifty
years of letting their eyes drift over tales of brutality in their
morning papers, Americans were taking notice. In May,
when *The Crisis* finally published White's findings about
Estill Springs and Fayetteville, another sickening multiple
lynching came to light, in Georgia's Lowndes and Brooks
counties. Sidney Johnson, a black prisoner on lease, killed
the white farmer he was leased to, one Hampton Smith,
and escaped to nearby Valdosta. White mobs gathered and
for two days rushed through the two counties on a wave
of blood, killing at least six African Americans, including
Mary Turner, nine months pregnant. She was hanged off a
bridge, then set afire. The fire did not kill her, though, so
the mob cut her open, stomped the fetus to death, and then
murdered her. No charges were filed.

With Johnson and White at the center of the action now,
the NAACP began to transform its anti-lynching efforts from
a moral advocacy campaign aimed mostly at whites into a
mouthpiece for black demands. Johnson's suave urbanity
had pulled Ovington into his confidence just as the demands
of Du Bois and his imperious style began to fray her friendship. For his part, Du Bois had moved past his suspicions
of Johnson as a Tuskegee man and saw instead their shared

connection to Atlanta University and the exalted Talented Tenth. With White and his modern impulse developing into the terrier counterpoint to Johnson's smooth approach, and Du Bois using *The Crisis* as a rallying point for the race, these three men formed a new working culture at the NAACP. By relying more and more—and visibly so—on its black executives for action and direction, the organization built credibility among black Americans.

Through the early part of the summer of 1918, Johnson took the fight past the newspapers, to Washington, where he introduced White to the corridors of political power, putting him into meetings with members of the House so he could recount his Estill Springs adventure in person, and involving him in the drafting of an anti-lynching bill by Missouri representative Leonidas Dyer. For all this grooming, though, it was White's next undercover trip, in August, to investigate the Lowndes and Brooks counties lynchings, that Johnson called "his first important job in this work."

In a 1929 piece for the *American Mercury*, called "I Investigate Lynchings," White sets the scene with color—and a stretch of the truth. He claims he arrived "shortly after the butchery," which is true in only the most relative sense since three months had passed between the events and his visit. Still, it's likely tensions were as high as he says they were in that rural patch of Georgia. The lynchings had continued; the town remained as prosperous, its citizens as blighted. Having been tipped off that the general store's owner was a ringleader of the Turner lynching, White went in, bought something small, and then turned on his traveling-salesman charm, chatting about war news and the weather until he sensed his mark was ready. He brought up the lynching. The owner balked. White hurriedly assured him that he had "great admiration for the manly spirits the men of the town had exhibited." At which the man sat him down, handed him a Coca-Cola,

and told him the whole story, right down to the details of
how they'd killed the mother and child. The list of names
White drew out of him included many of the town's leading men. The next day, some of them took him to the place
where they'd done it. "I shall never forget," wrote White in a
1924 letter, "the morning when I stood where Mary Turner
was killed, her grave marked by an empty quart whisky bottle
with the stump of a cigar stuck in its mouth. . . ."

By the third day White had raised suspicions, and the
owner accused him of being a government agent, a charge
that White didn't deny. An African American from the town
came to his hotel that night and warned him that a group
of white men had said "something would happen" to White
if he stayed in town. He called the bluff: "I looked straight
into my informant's eyes and said, in as convincing a tone
as I could muster: 'You go back to the ones who sent you
and tell them this: that I have a damned good automatic and
I know how to use it.'" The counterthreat worked. Despite
"much passing and re-passing of the hotel" by locals, White
survived the night and headed straight to Atlanta. Producing his credentials from the *New York Post*, he secured an
interview with Governor Hugh Dorsey. Among the more
liberal Southern governors of the era, Dorsey, infuriated by
the ruse, claimed he was powerless to do anything about
Lowndes and Brooks counties, but he accepted White's findings and in years to come emerged as a vocal opponent of
lynching.

A few weeks later White was on the road again, now investigating forced-labor practices in Alabama, Georgia, Florida, Louisiana, Mississippi, Arkansas, and Tennessee, jump-
starting local NAACP branches along the way with speeches.
"I suspect he runs very real danger," Ovington wrote to Joel
Spingarn, "but I am glad to see that he goes ahead just the

same." White's first year on the job was a whirlwind: he traveled more than twelve thousand miles (recording all his expenses with the tidiness of a former cashier), investigated at least three other lynchings, published his first article outside *The Crisis* (a piece for the *New Republic* on forced-labor practices), and became the most requested NAACP speaker.

To do it all, White had to navigate the arbitrary and constantly expanding absurdities of segregation: the white and colored Pullman cars, the separate entrances and facilities that could be challenging enough for any Northern black come South to keep track of. Baltimore passed the nation's first law enforcing residential segregation only in 1910. To all this White added the factor of playing the role of a white man, on top of which, after convincing whites that he was one of them, he would often go to the other side of the tracks and convince the black population that he was really one of *them.* Any slip, any misreading of the signs or lack of attention to detail, could easily have cost White his life. It was a staggering task that surely required extreme mental discipline. Its many facets and layers of reality forged White's identity as a black activist even as it hardened his self-reliance as a human being highly aware of the vagaries and shortcomings of racial identity. Racism and segregation offended White less because of how it affected him as a black man but because of how it reduced him as a man.

The next year, 1919, was even busier. In an upbeat January letter to influential board member Joel Spingarn, Ovington describes 70 Fifth Avenue as "a great big, hustling office now," staffed with secretaries paid for mostly through the expanding base of local branches invigorated by White's travels. Whatever optimism Ovington had did not last long. Nineteen nineteen was a tragic and bizarre year that found not just America but the entire world seized in a postwar flux of ideology and power. The war had given bloody birth to the modern mind and new political orders, most important the Russian Revolution, triggering red scares throughout Europe and the United States. Amidst peace talks in Paris, labor unrest, housing shortages, and mass migrations set America on edge. Paranoia over communism led to Americans being shot for not standing for the national anthem, or arrested in the street for reading aloud the Declaration of Independence. In the South, representatives of both races warned that things were ready to blow. Not only the Talented Tenth had fought in Europe; average Joes had gone to France and been celebrated as heroes. Now the New Negro, a black everyman, had come home with his eyes opened and willing to fight. And fight he did. Twenty-five separate race riots erupted that year, and White was literally in the middle of some of them.

For six months he traveled from state to state, constantly on the move—Chattanooga on January 13; Nashville, January 15; New Orleans, January 17; undercover in Shubata, Mississippi, January 19, working on both the black and white sides of town to find the truth about a pre-Christmas lynching of four men; and on and on. At almost every stop there was a meeting with an NAACP branch or a group trying to start one, public meetings with standing-room-only crowds. In early February he attended the rigged trial of two white lynchers in Sheffield, Alabama, with Shillady, the two of them posing as journalists. As he went, White submitted articles to *The Dial* and *The Nation*, and wrote pieces for the *New York Evening Post*.

April and May he spent mostly in the North, in cities such as Pittsburgh, Cincinnati, and Indianapolis, where he may have engaged in the sort of dalliance men on the road are susceptible to. In a letter to White dated June 17, a certain "Miriam" discusses in quite flirty tones whether her father will let her make a trip to Atlantic City, where she will ostensibly meet him. When she tells him people are still talking about him in Indianapolis, she stops short of details, saying he "might have to buy a new hat"—a line that later shows up in White's own writings, though Miriam does not.

If he stopped for romance, it was only a short respite. He was off to Chicago for a few nights in June to infiltrate a local homeowners' meeting on the South Side, where plans were being made to exclude black families from buying houses—by violence if necessary. The city wanted only a spark to set it on fire, and it got it a month later on Sunday, July 27, when a young African American named Eugene Williams swam over an imaginary line in Lake Michigan that separated black and white at a South Side beach. Whites onshore threw rocks until one hit Williams, and he drowned. Violence began when a white policeman did not arrest the stone thrower. Although the situation calmed that evening, on Monday night it exploded. Labor problems in the packinghouses turned the white street-corner gangs of the stockyards into mobs that set upon blacks. Groups of whites drove shooting into black neighborhoods, and blacks shot back. The city went mad. Seventeen died that night. By Wednesday, when Mayor "Big Bill" Thompson called for the state militia, almost forty people had been killed.

Shillady and NAACP publicity director Herbert Seligman went to Chicago. White, who had been investigating lynchings in Florida and Georgia, then attending a meeting in Washington, arrived on August 6. The editor of the *Chicago Daily News* put him together with one of his reporters, the young Carl Sandburg, to visit neighborhoods on the South Side. White was shot at in front of the Binga Bank on Thirty-fifth Street by a man who assumed he was actually white.

With the worst of the violence over, White's efforts were aimed chiefly at assembling a united reaction from Chicago's black community, no easy task since what leadership there was ranged from inert to radical. Given the NAACP's growing public profile and strength, White saw his main job as bringing all the bickering parties under NAACP direction, which meant brushing off the philosophical debates of worthy people such as Ida Wells-Barnett. While he's been accused of sexism for this, and of demanding control for his organization and, by extension, himself, the frustration that comes through in his letters makes his urge for unity understandable. "Although," he wrote Ovington during the talks, "I am not much in the mood for writing tonight due to my spending two hours this afternoon listening to debates on totally irrelevant points instead of getting down to business by the people supposed to do the work here, I am writing to report progress to date."

That White pushed the NAACP to the top shouldn't surprise; this was his brand, his business. "Enemies of ours are closely watching us," he wrote Ovington as soon as he reached Chicago, "to see if we can and will make good, and if we don't then we might as well close up shop." Yet long before he ever came on the scene, the white leadership of the organization had been adamant about establishing the NAACP's primacy in national race matters. Any mania White had for his employer came as much from its corporate culture as from his own ambitions. Through the fall and into 1920, the black response to the Chicago riots did eventually form along the lines White advised. Chicago taught him the need to bring all things racial under the NAACP umbrella, but also that at the age of twenty-five he could sit at the head of a table.

The fierce climax to the year came on September 30, in Phillips County, Arkansas. Two whites raided a meeting of black sharecroppers trying to break out of peonage with a cooperative. Returning fire, the sharecroppers killed one of their attackers. The next day whites from the surrounding region launched a pogrom in the towns of Elaine and Helena, murdering at least twenty-five but perhaps as many as two hundred blacks. When National Guard troops finally arrived, they joined the killing spree. Three whites had been killed, but the chaos made an exact count of the black dead impossible. Sixty-seven blacks were tried, resulting in death penalties for twelve of them, some handed down after only two minutes of deliberation. No whites were arrested.

Walter White arrived in Arkansas early on October 12 to investigate. His first stop was the office of Governor Charles Brough, where he again posed as a *Chicago Daily News* reporter, down to a fake business card, and induced the governor to write him a letter of introduction that he would use the next day in Helena. As usual, White's account in "I Investigate Lynchings" and in his autobiography melt a little when compared even to the scant materials in the NAACP papers. In both pieces he makes it sound as if he stays in Elaine and Helena for several days, when the official travel record he submitted has him leaving Little Rock for Helena at 7 a.m. on October 14 and returning to Memphis the next day; and he blurs Elaine and Helena, placing West Cherry Street in both towns. Still, he had genuine apprehensions: "If you haven't received a telegram from me by Thursday night," he wrote Johnson on Wednesday, "it might be well for you to start a discrete inquiry . . ."

White confined his interviews there to local whites, and though he didn't gain much useful information, he did get one of his most famous stories. "Within half an hour of my arrival," he later wrote, "I had been asked by two shopkeepers, a restaurant waiter, and a ticket agent why I had come to Elaine, what my business was, and what I thought of the recent riot." Although his salesman skills put them off the scent long enough to get his work done, eventually a black man walking past him on the main street pulled him aside to deliver a warning that the whites knew who he was and were planning to lynch him. White went straight to the station and got on one of the two trains out of town that day, but he faced one more hurdle. The conductor gave him a funny look and asked why he was leaving "just when the fun is going to start. . . . 'There's a damned yellow nigger down here passing for white and the boys are going to get him. . . .' No matter what the distance, I shall never take as long a train ride as that one seemed to be." White made it back to Memphis alive, and very relieved.

*

White traveled another 26,000 miles traveled in 1919, and displayed more heroics, but not everyone at 70 Fifth Avenue was thrilled with him. Mary White Ovington, for example, was never fully convinced. "I never yet have known a conspicuously short man who did not seem conceited," she wrote about White. "I'm afraid they can't help it—they must learn it as boys when they have to stand up against bigger boys." Although Du Bois said White "could be one of the most charming of men," the assistant secretary struck him as "self-centered and egotistical" and "often absolutely unscrupulous."

It's true that White often played situations in whatever way best suited his needs. For instance, he used the fake press credentials Villard had given him as cover in Estill Springs in order to gain access to Governor Dorsey in Atlanta, angering Villard in the process. Then he not only promoted the meeting afterward but wrote an account for *The Crisis*. Was he playing a reporter with Dorsey, or was he a real one? Or was *he* the real story? In Sheffield, Alabama, he posed as a reporter but then wrote a story about it. When he presented his *Daily News* credentials to Governor Brough in Arkansas, who was he exactly?

This ability to exist as many different things at once— simply another aspect of his upbringing—was rarely seen as a talent by his white colleagues and employers, most of whom offered him at best cautious admiration. There was something tricky about him, and lightweight. To White, though, there was no proper way to fight white oppression. He came to the NAACP not as an ideologue but as someone who got a better job offer. His only philosophy was what worked, and his sometimes imprecise operating methods showed that he'd learned to navigate his complicated racial identity through expedience. Instead of hiding behind the veil Du Bois described in *The Souls of Black Folk*, a haunted, divided soul, White had wrapped himself in the veil, becoming at once black, white, neither, and both, depending on what he needed to be at the time but always telling himself that whatever he did, he did for his race. Doing the thing that worked now made more sense to him than operating from a dug-in position. Flexibility was also at the core of a faster-moving world and the increasing importance of media. Did it really matter in Sheffield whether he was posing as a reporter or really acting as one, as long as he got the story out as quickly and as effectively as possible? This was total war, and it had to be won no matter what. Besides, in 1917 the NAACP had hired a woman to investigate lynchings under the guise of a reporter for the *New York Evening Post*, and even Johnson now encouraged White to use the shield of the press when possible. So the cavils of Shillady and Villard had more to do with control than ethics.

Expedience and flexibility are strong qualities for a lobbyist or politician. Not surprisingly, in time White would become a master at both, but his interest in quick solutions would increasingly cause him problems as he took on more cases. At times it made him susceptible to better strategists such as a white lawyer named C. P. Dam, who in 1918 claimed to be setting up hearings on lynchings on behalf of his friend, Iowa senator William Kenyon. Although the NAACP had no need to throw in with this slight effort, White cooperated, giving away much more of his group's strategy than he needed to. Expediency could also prove damaging to the NAACP's image, as the politics of necessity threw the organization into relations with moderate but hardly enlightened Southern organizations, such as the Law and Order League and the Commission of Interracial Cooperation, which looked to some like compromise.

Still, if white America was unnerved by Walter White, all the better for him. His growing fame came from doing exactly that, and despite his deceptive skin color he had no trouble in these early years establishing his credibility among African Americans. Black men and women filled the halls and lodges and churches where he appeared, laughing along with him at his tales of fooling the white man on their behalf. With these stories White created a character, a skinny young black trickster who walked into the teeth of danger in the name of justice and who came out not only alive but laughing. "Trickster is a non-heroic male," writes Lewis Hyde in *Trickster Makes This World*, "If by 'hero' we mean someone who muscles his way through the ranks of his enemies, whose stamina and grit overcome all odds, who perseveres and suffers and wins, then trickster is a non-heroic male. Nor is he that ascetic male, the one who develops the muscles of self-restraint, mastering himself instead of others. The lithe and small-bodied escape artist, he doesn't win the way the big guys do, but he doesn't suffer the way they do, either, and he enjoys pleasures they find too risky."

The point of White's stories was not to chronicle his actions by the standards of current media scrutiny. These were unashamedly self-aggrandizing, name-dropping, chest-thumping tales of audacity and bravery, intended to establish his authority and inspire action. With his high-pitched voice, love of a joke, and relentless energy, his speeches were entertainment of a high order. When the audience left, they told their neighbors the stories they'd heard from this character Walter White, who tricked out lynchers for the NAACP. Those kinds of people weren't just unconcerned that he could play on the borders, they were thrilled by it, because it had a precedent in black culture.

Like all things about White, the personal layer must be addressed. Did he do all this to be famous? His genuine commitment aside, most likely yes. He clearly loved it. But fame was necessary for him to be heard, and he wasn't waiting for it to be bestowed on him; he needed to claim it. To gain public status in the black community, as the writings of Henry Louis Gates, Roger Abrahams, Valérie Smitherson, and other socio-linguists suggest, White needed to be *bad*. His stories had to be dynamic and lively. They had to show him signifying on the white man, misdirecting him, tricking him, mocking him, being a many-layered person in the white world. He had to boast. Boring, fact-checked reportage from a self-effacing reporter was not about to rally black America in the Jazz Age or give the NAACP the zip it needed to fend off the appeal of Marcus Garvey. To do that, White needed to display verbal dexterity, as later would Dr. King, Malcolm X, or any figure in hip-hop culture today. "White was one of the best talkers I have ever heard," said his successor at the NAACP, Roy Wilkins. As Albert Murray might say, White had to swing his stories, and since there's no evidence he ever approached his reportage on the lynchings themselves with anything less than professionalism, he made himself the subject of the swing. Despite his two novels, four works of nonfiction, and countless articles, these stories of his adventures as an undercover spy for the NAACP, told to black audiences, are White's greatest, and completely lost, artistic contribution.

*

Just before the Red Summer of 1919 took fire, the NAACP had hosted an Anti-Lynching Conference in May at Carnegie Hall in New York. Speaking before the 2,500 delegates, James Weldon Johnson delivered his famous statement that racial problems in America were a matter of "saving black men's bodies and white men's souls." The conference, judged a great success, closed with three resolutions for the NAACP: to secure a federal anti-lynching law; to organize state committees to work toward anti-lynching legislation on the state level; and to go forward with an aggressive national campaign of fundraising and advertising.

As sincere and committed as John Shillady may have been to overseeing this program, his tenure was brutally cut short on the streets of Austin, Texas, in August 1919. Denied meetings with Governor William P. Hobby as well as the state attorney general regarding attempts to prohibit the NAACP from operating in the state, Shillady was then hunted down and beaten by a gang of white men. The attack shattered him physically, but its most devastating effects were psychological. He resigned in 1920, broken in spirit, leaving room now for the elevation of James Weldon Johnson to head the NAACP. Judgment on Shillady was generally harsh, with even Arthur Spingarn accusing him of cowardice, but it speaks well of White that he offered only his sympathies. More than once, only luck had kept him from the same fate.

The Elaine massacre marks a transition in the anti-lynching campaign as well as in White's career. The widespread social violence of 1919 required a response from the NAACP beyond public relations and lobbying. Johnson, now at the helm, followed through on the resolutions of the Anti-Lynching Conference by pushing the Anti-Lynching Bill, introduced by Representative L. C. Dyer of Missouri, to the top of the agenda. The gruesome violence of the last two years had provided White and Johnson with more than enough sensational fodder, and important cases such as Elaine demanded long-term management. So White, a new public face and a hidden weapon at the same time, shifted to the managerial role he'd performed in Chicago. Working with Scipio Jones, the savvy black lawyer brought in to handle things on the ground in Arkansas, White now began four years on the case, with incessant strategizing, fund-raising, and creating publicity. He spent most of 1920 on the road throughout the North, raising funds, orchestrating the Elaine case, and assisting in Washington when needed.

His active investigations, though, were by no means over. The reemergent Ku Klux Klan made its effect known in the 1920 election between Republican Warren Harding and Democrat James Cox. While content in most places with intimidation, in Ocoee, Florida, the Klan struck violently against a successful black landowner named Moses Norman, who attempted to vote despite Klan warnings. The mob beat Norman, then followed him to the home of his friend July Perry, where they not only set fire to the Perry home but twenty-two other black homes and buildings, including a school. First reports claimed that five blacks were killed.

On November 5, three days after this election-day terrorism, White arrived in Orlando. Dusting off an old trick, he convinced a cab driver that he was in the market for an orange grove and soon came to Ocoee, a town still smoldering. Just then, as he relates in his report, "the last colored family of Ocoee was leaving with their goods piled high on a motor truck with six colored children on top. White children stood around and jeered the Negroes who were leaving, threatening them with burning if they did not hurry up and get away." Hiding behind his cover story, White was able to talk with white townspeople who described how African Americans had been shot as they ran out of burning buildings. In front of the post office, one man told him, "I don't know exactly how many niggers were killed but I do know that 56 were burned up—I killed 17 myself." Given the treacherous conditions, White secured no sworn affidavits, but in December he took his findings to the Justice Department and testified along with Johnson and field secretary William Pickens before a House committee.

Harding's election and a new Congress raised hopes that Dyer's anti-lynching bill had a chance for passage. Like the year before, White spent most of the first half of 1921 in the North, operating between New York and Washington and turning down a request from Chicagoan Oscar DePriest—who in 1928 would be elected as the first African American from a Northern state to the House of Representatives—to investigate Klan activity in Chicago. Johnson's hard legislative push was a canny move for the NAACP. No matter their geography, politics, income, or skin color, African Americans backed the Dyer Bill. The template for all anti-lynching bills that received NAACP support, it made a lynching by three or more people a federal crime and provided fines and jail time for local officials who either failed to stop a lynching or did not pursue prosecution of the lynchers.

When the bill had first been brought up in 1918, it had not had the full support of the NAACP. The organization's president and founding member, Moorfield Storey, an aged Brahmin lawyer who linked the NAACP to its abolitionist forebears by having been secretary to Senator Charles Sumner, had advised the organization to pull back because of concerns over the constitutionality of what defined a lynching.

Now Storey relented, and Johnson and White found a higher gear. Operating as best they could in segregated Washington, D.C., they worked the halls of Congress, talking strategy and lobbying with Dyer for passage of the bill, issuing press releases, organizing testimony, petitioning the White House, raising money—all of it making the NAACP the most visible force behind the first cause to unify African Americans nationally. By May their deft brokering of competing bills made Dyer optimistic about its chances.

Just then, May 30, 1921, the final spasm of post-war racial violence played out in Tulsa, Oklahoma. A young black shoeshine named Dick Rowlands accidentally stepped on the foot of Sarah Page, a seventeen-year-old elevator operator, sending the elevator into motion. Page lurched forward, and when Rowlands reached out to steady her, the girl ran from the elevator, screaming that she'd been assaulted. Rowlands was arrested. Tulsa woke the next day to rumors of a lynching that night, and as the rumors mounted, groups of armed African Americans, many of whom were World War I veterans, went to the jail resolved to protect Rowlands. That evening, fueled by rumors that Rowlands had been taken, one such group confronted a throng of an estimated two thousand whites. The resulting gunfight left ten whites and two blacks dead and touched off the worst race riot in American history. On the morning of June 1, white mobs spread through the Greenwood section of Tulsa, burning, looting, and shooting. Blacks were rounded up and held at the fairgrounds and other locations as whites looted their homes. Somewhere between seventy-five and two hundred African Americans were killed, and forty-four blocks of Greenwood were destroyed.

Within six hours of hearing the news, Walter White was on his way, entering the city on June 2. He claims in "I Investigate Lynchings" that "the excitement was at its peak," but if the worst was over, calm was by no means restored. In a piece published that June in *The Nation*, White says he was "sworn in as a special deputy in Tulsa." He spins the tale out further in an article for the *American Mercury*, narrating a dramatic scene in which he's deputized into a white posse under the guise of a reporter. As he waits to get into a car, a man seems to recognize him, even mentioning the NAACP. "As coolly as I could," he wrote later, "the circumstances being what they were, I took a cigarette from my case and lighted it, trying to keep my hand from betraying my nervousness." The two men exchange a loaded gaze, like the one he shared with the conductor in Elaine, Arkansas, until they all pile in. "It is hardly necessary to add that all that night, assigned to the same car with this man and his four companions, I maintained a considerable vigilance."

Something along these lines must have happened, but saying which version is closer to the truth would be utter speculation. White closes the story in "I Investigate Lynchings" by noting that a Tulsa paper threatened to sue him for "criminal libel" after he published his account, ". . . but nothing came of it after my willingness to defend it was indicated." In that light it's noteworthy that the story doesn't appear in his autobiography.

Secret agent, strategist, and now a familiar face on Capitol Hill, White was earning a reputation in Washington power circles as "a go-getter, a politician, a breezy, hearty good-fellow," as Garland Fund chairman and later ACLU founder Roger Baldwin put it. He liked a stiff drink, always looked on the bright side, and, as a friend later said, "the first thing he did was always to call you by your first name and that made you feel rather as if you were intimate." Clearly the qualities of the Life Insurance Temperament were transferable to Congress. Now, with the legislative work rolling forward, Johnson sent White on a mission to help shore up the NAACP on another front, broadening the assistant secretary's world and planting the seeds for his next incarnation.

*

As much as the years 1918 and 1919 brought terror for African Americans, they also shook the edifice of white, colonial power that ruled much of the world's darker populations. This was due, ironically enough, in no small part to the same man who turned a blind eye to racial terror in America, Woodrow Wilson. Good character, though, is not a requisite for achieving good in the world, as even White's story proves. In the Grand Hotel, a short walk from the Hotel Crillion and the Paris peace talks, W. E. B. Du Bois had convened the first Pan-African Conference, a successor in many ways to the Pan-African Congress he had attended in London in 1900. With most of its fifty-eight delegates from the United States and the Caribbean, the conference demanded that the freedoms and self-determination of Wilson's Fourteen Points, set forth at the peace conference, be extended to the world's black populations. Although largely symbolic, Du Bois's conference had further entrenched him and the NAACP as the established channel of black expression, strengthening their hand against the appeals of Marcus Garvey.

A dark-skinned Jamaican émigré, thick-set and extravagant, Garvey challenged the theoretical and political strategies of the NAACP with his populist "Back to Africa" movement. His organization, the United Negro Improvement Association (UNIA) spoke powerfully and directly to the desire for self-determination by soliciting investment from all levels of black society, throughout the world, in his shipping company, the Black Star Line, and advocating a degree of self-segregation that presaged Du Bois's later position. Civil rights and equality were not Garvey's concern.

Whether a con or a victim of poor management, Black Star failed, and Garvey eventually fell from grace, convicted in 1924 of mail fraud. Until then, though, UNIA and the NAACP battled for the heart of Harlem. Compared to Garvey's promise of self-help, dividends, and attractive uniforms, Johnson and White's sharp focus on anti-lynching legislation may have appeared a narrow agenda to some. But Johnson's "black bodies and white souls" proclamation invested the effort with a philosophical heft and an understanding of reality that UNIA did not have: civil rights would not be restored to black Americans until the majority of white Americans respected the integrity of the black body and understood the value of black lives to be at least comparable to their own.

Du Bois disliked Garvey intensely and used *The Crisis* to express his contempt, but the fight had many fronts and editorials were not enough to maintain the NAACP in its prime leadership role. Embroiled in his own internal difficulties with the board regarding control of *The Crisis*, Du Bois petitioned the NAACP to underwrite a second Pan-African Conference to reassert its international position and advance its own platform of Pan-African unity. The board agreed, and in August 1921 Du Bois and White set sail for London, but only after White worked out a slight difficulty with his passport. Whether concerned out of vanity or practicality, he received permission from the State Department to change his complexion on the passport from "dark" to "fair."

Once in London, White handled logistics for the meetings there while the historian Rayford Logan, at the time just twenty-four and recently demobilized from the army, and Jessie Fauset, literary editor of *The Crisis*, dealt with those in Paris and Brussels. White performed adequately under the gaze of the great Du Bois, twenty-five years his senior. He negotiated the details of the conference opening despite fierce politicking among continental and English delegates, and made a futile attempt with Du Bois to persuade British leaders such as Sidney Webb and Norman Angell of the Labour party to condemn their nation's colonial system. During the conference he delivered a speech on the anti-lynching campaign and was a vocal part of the American delegation as it helped Du Bois direct the final resolutions toward an emphasis on self-determination in Africa. The heavy lifting of philosophies, though, was not among his duties. With his ability to engage and amuse now well practiced in Washington, White spent much of his time in any number of elegant sitting rooms, meeting with the likes of H. G. Wells, author of *War of the Worlds* and then a highly influential socialist, and J. A. Hobson, editor of the *Manchester Guardian*, trying to steer them to public statements of support for the NAACP's anti-lynching work.

Although White would always maintain an international sensibility as secretary of the NAACP, devoting time and energy in the post–World War II era to global issues, this first trip abroad did more for White than create that sentiment. Four years earlier he hadn't been allowed into a meeting with the Atlanta Board of Education; now he was shaking hands with some of the great figures of the age, breathing an entirely different sort of air. He'd given himself over to the NAACP body, mind, and soul in that time, and made his name known, but those around him—Du Bois and Johnson, especially—were more than simply lobbyists. Like H. G. Wells and White's new friend, the singer Roland Hayes, whom he met in London, they were artists, making use of their minds, not just their wits or management skills. They had access to fascinating people on every continent. They changed the culture as much as the headlines. The trickster had made him who he was, but White returned from Europe ready for a new role.

CHAPTER FOUR

At the Center of the Harlem Renaissance

ᔕ January and February of 1922 crowned White's first four years in New York. After Europe, much of the fall of 1921 had been spent in Washington, securing votes for the Dyer Bill, all of which paid off in significant triumph when it passed the House 230 to 119 on January 26. Then, on February 15, White married Gladys Powell, his stenographer at the NAACP office, whom Langston Hughes called "the most beautiful brown woman in New York." Mary White Ovington described her to Joel Spingarn as "a statuesque creature, a bronze Galetia," though her admiration was only skin deep. Powell "would have attracted me the least," she then sniped.

To some it was an odd match, the tall, haughty beauty paired with someone Ovington deemed "a small, insignificant looking man, and with a poor delivery." But paring away her distaste, the attractions are obvious. Riding high, White and his prospects were only pointing up. He had guts and style, always wore a sharp suit, and his friends were fabulous. Gladys, on the other hand, was no less than Walter deserved for all that. Lovely and talented, the inheritor of a voice worthy of her father who'd founded the Powell Jubilee Singers, she had come to the NAACP in the winter of 1920 after working as a secretary in the War Department, then appearing in the chorus of a handful of Broadway musicals. If she had any remaining dreams of singing professionally, White made sure she tucked them away—Gladys was pregnant almost immediately after the wedding. Her job, for better and usually for worse, was to be the wife of Walter White.

While it's possible to pull apart the threads of what White accomplished over the next five years, separating out his NAACP work from all he did amidst the Harlem Renaissance fails to convey not just his peripatetic nature but how integrated it all was in his mind, how he became, according to David Levering Lewis, one of the six "midwives" of the movement. Standing on the platform he'd built through his investigations, over the next five years White began to claim for himself some of that fame he had created for the NAACP, asserting himself socially and artistically in a variety of directions, exploiting his position in the organization to promote himself as much as he freely used his own writing and connections to promote civil rights and the NAACP. To him it was all of a piece.

Then, as now, this struck many as somehow craven. But the utter selflessness we expect from someone who devotes his or her life to a cause is often at odds with the realities of human nature. Nowhere to this point had White ever claimed he'd made a lifelong commitment to the NAACP; what he had committed to was the cause of black civil rights. In Atlanta he'd displayed an unseemly coyness about his future, publicly mulling his options like a man on the prowl for a better date. But once aboard, he'd put in four years at the NAACP, learning the ropes—and risking his life.

Now his personal ambitions came forward. Pushing thirty, married with a child on the way, set up in a new Harlem apartment at 90 Edgecombe Avenue, White was no longer a boy, no matter how impossible it was for him with his blond hair to grow a full mustache. Even counting the raise to $3,000 a year that the board voted him upon his marriage, money was tight. Ambition, he had learned from the likes of Herndon and Perry, was not just good, it was his responsibility. The white grandees surrounding him at the NAACP could only have whet his appetite for more in life. Wasn't Du Bois himself, the great philosopher, always working some new project to help pay the exorbitant cost of his daughter's English boarding school tuition? Fame and finances would lead the man who would later be known as "Mr. NAACP" to consider a number of schemes and opportunities between 1924 and 1928 that would have meant leaving the organization. There's no evidence that he was unhappy working at the NAACP. It was his power base, where he wed his creative and personal endeavors to his NAACP work to such an extent that they became almost indistinguishable. White simply didn't let his job there limit what he desired to achieve. His hunger for attention and rewards helped create the Harlem Renaissance and encouraged it to bloom for as long as it did.

*

Although cultural movements are rarely born on a specific date, at a particular hour, the Harlem Renaissance includes a lunch in the spring of 1922 as one of its many moments of conception. James Weldon Johnson brought White along to a meeting with H. L. Mencken, the acid editor of *The Smart Set* magazine. Mencken lived in a state of eternal dyspepsis, venting his dislike of nearly everyone and everything in pages of tonic prose. A public champion of writers such as Theodore Dreiser and Sinclair Lewis, he did so more often in hopes that they would beat down whatever form of ignorance currently offended his gadfly sense of intellectual supremacy than that they would create something artistically glorious. Most likely Johnson had introduced White and Mencken years earlier since there are letters between them going back to 1920—Mencken's diatribes against the Bourbon South thrill the starstruck White, who labors to keep up with his eloquent friend. One can see the beads of sweat in such lines as "I am wondering if there isn't a good deal of innate meanness in my makeup when I so greatly enjoyed your philippic on 'The Sahara of Bozart'?"

In a series of letters after this 1922 lunch, Mencken asked White what he thought of *Birthright*, a recent novel about black life by T. S. Stribling, a white author. White sent him a response that he himself calls "lengthy and painfully erudite," discussing the shortcomings of whites writing about black America. Mencken then pulled the cord on the lightbulb over White's head: Why didn't White write a novel himself?

Not long after this, White sat down with two friends, both black women, Jessie Fauset and Nella Larsen. A Phi Beta Kappa graduate of Cornell who was nine years White's senior, Fauset had been literary editor of *The Crisis* since 1919 and by this meeting had already taken two important figures of the Harlem Renaissance under her wing: the young Langston Hughes and the novelist Jean Toomer. Although she'd host one of the primary salons of the period with her sister Helen Lanning, and liked to dance, the poet Claude McKay called her "prim school-marmish and stilted." More of a wren even than Fauset, the fair-skinned Larsen was White's social friend. The two had met during his courtship of Gladys and continued to see each other at the many events starting to take place at the 135th Street branch of the New York Public Library, where Larsen was a junior assistant librarian in the children's book section. After discussing *Birthright* and Mencken's advice, all three decided to take up his challenge.

That September, as the Elaine case dragged on and lobbying continued in the Senate for passage of the Dyer Bill,
White accepted Mary White Ovington's offer of her small
country house in Great Barrington, Massachusetts. With
Gladys eight months pregnant, it must have been a happy
respite from the city. But in a troubling preview of their married life, White spent the lion's share of their holiday at the
typewriter. "Today we have been here one week," he wrote
Johnson. "Not counting last Tuesday and as I haven't done
my day's stint as yet, in six days I have written slightly more
than 35,000 words on my novel" (in rough exchange, 125
pages). Twelve feverish days at the keys had produced the
first draft of *Fire in the Flint*.

In the story, the young black doctor Kenneth Harper,
based on White's friend Dr. Louis T. Wright, returns to his
small hometown in Georgia after attending Atlanta University, earning his medical degree, and putting in a tour of duty
in France during World War I. Although he hopes to keep his
nose clean and quietly set up his own practice, step by step
Harper falls deeper into the town's dark soul. Right off he
runs afoul of the other black doctor in town and sees that
the white doctor is a fool. A black man is shot when his wife
is found in bed with a white man, but Harper is warned by
the Klan to keep quiet. Then, while Harper is out of town
trying to set up the sort of agricultural collective that the
whites of Phillips County, Arkansas, destroyed, Harper's
sister is gang-raped. His brother Bob kills two of the rapists
and is lynched. Filled with hatred now for whites, Harper is
nonetheless persuaded by a white woman to come tend to
her daughter while the husband is out of town. When Harper
is seen at the house, it's assumed he's having an affair with
the woman, and our hero is lynched.

As it would eventually be published, the book conveys
the manic energy of those twelve days at the typewriter, full

of passion and intensity but too hurried to settle into the ease of telling that marks a confident writer. It's stiff, like a dancer who knows the steps but has no rhythm, relentlessly driving home the daily indignities and horrors of black life in the rural South without ever fully creating a world or realizing its characters. The genius of *Fire in the Flint*, such as it is, comes from the fact that never before, without deference or pleading, had a book displayed the moral and intellectual degradation of white America through the eyes of an angry, disgusted black world.

In time *Fire in the Flint* would prompt controversy, but it wasn't quite ready as White continued to tinker with it in the very busy fall of 1922. In October, Gladys gave birth to their daughter Jane, who would—luckily for her—favor her mother's tall, theatrical beauty. But soon after this happy beginning came the frustrating realization that years of lobbying and politicking on the Dyer Bill were about to fall short. Democratic filibustering and a lack of key Republican support kept the bill from reaching the Senate floor after the November midterm elections, and the prospects down the line weren't good. America was not prepared to demand this level of moral accountability on behalf of all its citizens. And yet after the public debate surrounding the bill, the number of lynchings in America would drop in 1923 to thirty-three, from sixty-four in 1921 and fifty-seven in 1922. Whether or not Johnson and White ever admitted this to themselves, the true value of anti-lynching legislation proved to be in the public discussion that drove home its moral message. A single stroke of the pen would not end the barbarity of lynching in America.

But the pen could help black America triumph in other ways. Through the fall and winter, the elements of the Harlem Renaissance percolated. Claude McKay's *Harlem Shadows* was published, and the poet, a lifelong malcontent who seemed to burn bridges even as he crossed them, made plans to move to Harlem upon return from his tour of the infant Soviet Union. Portly and proper Countee Cullen took honorable mention in the Witter Bynner Undergraduate Poetry competition, while on every corner Fauset, Cullen, influential NAACP board member Joel Spingarn (former chairman of the Columbia University comparative literature department), and Howard University professor Alain Locke sang the praises of a poet named Langston Hughes, currently sailing as a messboy on the *SS Malone*. James Weldon Johnson moved some of his regular meetings of artists and thinkers from the Algonquin Hotel up to his place on 135th Street. Fletcher Henderson formed his first band, and soon his refined take on Louis Armstrong's Chicago sound would become the score for the Harlem Renaissance. The all-black Broadway show *Liza* kicked off the Charleston craze. And, most important, under the direction of its visionary white librarian Ernestine Rose, the 135th Street branch of the New York Public Library offered itself as the cultural center of the community with a sensitive and innovative program of readings and lectures.

Gladys and Walter, meanwhile, were very much in the middle of it all, part of a whole other universe than the deadly rural hamlets he'd been investigating. While Du Bois may have returned from Europe with Pan-African visions, White had acquired a more sophisticated veneer that his twelve days of typing in the Berkshires would hopefully reinforce. Folded into the social life of Harlem at parties hosted by his mentor Johnson and NAACP board member Charles Studin, and with fresh memories of his recent wanders through the very sort of London drawing rooms his mother's stuffy, pseudo-Victorian parlor aspired to, White began to entertain. Partying, after all, was what the ex-frat boy had been most famous for, and he'd be famous for it again as he and Gladys showed a quick talent as hosts. A fizzy dinner partner, White was up to date on everyone and everything; genial, gentlemanly, full of opinions and exciting stories, "an enthusiastic young dilettante." Walter and Gladys made their apartment one of Uptown's premier meeting places. After a February appearance at the library book club by the author Clement Wood, the Whites held a dinner and reception for him, pouring the gin even with four-month-old Jane down the hall. (White had reviewed Wood's book for *The Nation* and, in his accustomed bold fashion, had then asked the author for advice on his own writing.)

As Jean Toomer's virtuoso novel *Cane* hit the stores in 1923 and the *Pittsburgh Courier* serialized White's lynching pieces from *The Crisis*, Walter kept at it with *Fire in the Flint*. He was encouraged by a meeting with George Doran, whose publishing house had brought out books by, among others, Arnold Toynbee, Arthur Conan Doyle, and P. G. Wodehouse. Through the summer all signs pointed to a happy ending. In June, Doran's associate editor Eugene Saxton wrote White that "the possibilities seem strongly in favor of our making you an offer for it." White then hit the typewriter again to address some of Saxton's concerns, including giving greater depth and complexity to the character of the white Judge Stephenson, arguably the best-drawn of the cast. As an author, White didn't fear criticism, nor did he seem to take editing as a personal affront. What came next, though, was. After a tepid response in late July to White's second draft, Saxton finally admitted in August that Doran would not publish the novel because it leaned "exclusively on one side of the case." In fact, Doran had asked his friend Irvin Cobb, an author of sentimental Southern humor, to give his opinion of the manuscript. Not surprisingly, Cobb had been offended by the pages.

Through August, White and Saxton exchanged an interesting series of letters as Saxton manfully defended a weak position: "Personally," he wrote, "I should be entirely willing to have ninety-five percent of all you say remain in the book if there were some moderately fair presentation of the white man's case." Was that to say, a defense of lynching? Of oppression and gang rape and summary justice? Not all white men called that their "case." The book's power derived in large part from the way its author demolished preconceptions and made white readers see themselves as they were seen by African Americans. While it can be argued that Saxton was trying to push White to a better work of art and less a piece of propaganda, it's worth asking whether Saxton would have required such balance from Upton Sinclair or Dreiser. More likely, confronted with an ugly portrait of members of their race, Doran and Saxton reflexively defended them.

White easily and graciously fended off each of Saxton's complaints in his replies, offering to do further revision and even suggesting that their letters be published as a foreword to the book to offer context and a voice for the opposing side. The desperation seeps through White's words—Boni and Liveright was set to publish Jessie Fauset's *There Is Confusion* in the spring, and White had surely wanted to be first. But more, there is anger: "It is not that I sought to do injustice to the white man, nor was there any lack of desire to give the white man's side of the case. Certainly, I think he has a case but, by all that is holy, all we've had is his side. . . . The South has so dehumanized and brutalized itself by its policy of repression of the Negro that my white characters are true to life. They *are* ineffectual. They *are* depraved. They *are* rotten. . . ."

As Joel Spingarn solicited readings from influential Southern liberals, White saw what was coming. He reached out to Mencken for a reading at Knopf but also solicited H. G. Wells for a promise to look at the book in galleys

Although White's literary pretensions fizzled
by the late 1920s, his energy and connections
had helped stimulate the Harlem Renaissance.
(Library of Congress)

in hopes that would influence Doran. It was "not a great
piece of writing," he wrote the best-selling author, "but it
is an honest and sincere attempt to give a picture which
has hitherto never been shown." Wells did not reply until
years later. Although Will Alexander of the Commission of
Interracial Cooperation eventually expressed his support of
the book, it was no use. On October 8 Saxton rejected *Fire
in the Flint*.

Something better was waiting, though. His pleas to
Mencken heard, White sent the manuscript over to Knopf

on the 18th at his friend's instruction and met with Blanche
Knopf, wife of the publisher Alfred, four days later. By December, Knopf had accepted *Fire in the Flint* for publication
in fall of 1924. The awful journey with Doran and the many
tough readings he'd received from Mencken and others had
brought White down to earth—for the moment. "I have no
illusions regarding the literary style of my novel," he wrote
Blanche Knopf. "I know it has many gaucheries, many inept
and crude phrases." In the months to come, he would work
on his fiction, generally improving it. His humility, though,
would suffer.

*

Through the whole struggle in 1923 to get *Fire in the Flint*
into print, White's star at the NAACP shone brightly. All
his hard work on the Elaine massacre case, along with the
local maneuverings of Scipio Jones, finally culminated in
the landmark Supreme Court decision *Moore v. Dempsey*,
which reversed the convictions of six of the men and established the precedent that defendants were entitled not only
to a trial but to a *fair* trial. In his opinion, Justice Oliver
Wendell Holmes wrote, "if in fact a trial is dominated by a
mob, so that there is an actual interference with the course
of justice, there is a departure from due process of law. . . ."
Moorfield Storey, who argued the case, credited White for
his direction, and Johnson agreed. "The handling of the Arkansas cases at the National Office has been almost entirely
in the hands of Mr. White," he reported to the board, "who
has performed the work with a great deal of intelligence and
skill."

It hadn't been easy. White's Talented Tenth orientation
and his focus on doing things the NAACP way caused friction
between him and Scipio Jones. After the ruling, Jones rec-

ommended that the six remaining defendants plead guilty to lesser charges in order to reduce their terms, a plan White shot down with Storey's encouragement because it meant accepting guilt for a crime they did not commit. This decision has led some to cast White as cold-blooded and unconcerned about the human cost so long as the NAACP achieved greater glory, proving in turn that he was an elitist. A golden boy of the Talented Tenth, raised within a select segment of Black Atlanta, a known face on Capitol Hill and now an ever-brighter fixture on the Harlem scene, White in all ways personally and socially did define himself as "elite." He was not oblivious to the fact nor embarrassed by it, but he also saw it as relative and fluid.

One scene in *Fire in the Flint* reveals much about White's attitude toward social stratification within black society and his place in it. After the murder of the black cuckold, Reverend Wilson, the town's black preacher, comes to see Kenneth, who's disgusted by his broad sermonizing. To Kenneth he represents the worst stereotype of rural black clergy, but when Wilson sits down with him, the preacher drops the dialect and suddenly sounds like an AU grad. Kenneth is stunned. The poor black folks of Central City "don't want a preacher that's too far above them," says Wilson, "—they'll feel that they can't come to him and tell him their troubles if he's too highfalutin. I try to get right down to my folks, feel as they feel, suffer when they suffer, laugh with them when they laugh, and talk with them in language they can understand." Kenneth now takes to Wilson. "The simile of the protective device of the chameleon came to his [Kenneth's] mind. Yes, the Negro in the South had many things in common with the chameleon—he had to be able to change his color figuratively to suit the environment of the South in order to be allowed to stay alive."

Again, as he did in August 1906, White defines blackness in terms of himself—here, as a chameleon. Outward color is less a defining factor of blackness than how one *uses* his identity as an African American. In a variation on Du Bois's veil, blackness means the *necessity* to change color in order to survive, and the way White plays with black and white every day of his life is really just an extreme version of the signifying that other African Americans must do. To him, the ability to navigate the complexities of not just segregation but the emotional and physical realities of racial politics is what made him truly black. As solipsistic, self-serving, and even possibly accurate as this definition was, no matter what color White the chameleon changed into, what role he played, he always felt the profound responsibility that George White and Reverend Proctor had instilled in him as a requirement for inclusion in the black elite, distasteful as the idea of an "elite" might be to many. Pouring the drinks and making many of the introductions that created the Harlem Renaissance, focused all the while on his own interests and gladly accepting whatever perks came his way, White never wavered in his commitment to the cause of African-American advancement. It was his chosen business.

*

With its anti-lynching campaign scaled back in the wake of the Dyer Bill's defeat in the Senate, the NAACP spent most of these two years, 1923 and 1924, wrangling over its next direction, consolidating its gains, and feeding the creative ferment in black thought. Johnson and Du Bois spared no ink, never hesitated to make a phone call or drop a line if it could somehow advance a career, make a connection, or inspire a grand thought about the achievement of African-American artists. Surely it was a breath of fresh air after so much concentration on violent death and victimization, and it gave White an idea that reflects his unique vantage from the center of it all. His magazine pieces from this time—especially an abortive article on African art that Alfred Barnes, an idiosyncratic yet powerful collector and friend of Johnson, shot down with words such as "cheap" and "exploitation"—further prove that White was no scholar. They express a sense of how people should think rather than a critical exigesis. Heavily daubed with the ironic style of his friends Mencken and George Schuyler, White delivers impatient directives and bald observations. As a man of constant action, though, he saw what needed to be *done* with much better sight than what needed to be thought about. Looking out at all the exciting developments in Harlem, he decided they needed a corporate stamp, some kind of organization to flower. To this end he proposed to Alain Locke a "Negro Art Institute" for, as Locke would later put it, "the expert training and direction of Negro students." So natural an idea was this to Locke that to him it seemed "now a question of how soon and under what auspices." White solicited Johnson's thoughts, and Locke even drew up a provisional "Constitution of AMERICAN (NATIONAL) INSTITUTE OF NEGRO LETTERS, MUSIC AND ART" to use, it seems, for fund-raising. As Locke conceived it, the organization would have departments in Music, Drama, Literature and Folklore, Design and Painting, and Sculpture and African Crafts. Given its enormous scope, White's role would have been sizable, so this must be seen as an alternative to his position at the NAACP. The money never came through, however, leaving White still at 70 Fifth Avenue and the emergence of the arts in Harlem to explode rather than be nurtured.

That explosion happened in the spring of 1924. In her editorial process Jessie Fauset had not encountered the rough water that White had, so she beat him to the finish with her novel *There Is Confusion* that March. To celebrate, Charles Johnson, director of the Urban League, threw her a book party at the Civic Club that has come down through time as the moment when the Harlem Renaissance crystallized. The smartest names Harlem could offer graced the tables, laced with influential white publishers and editors such as Carl Van Doren and Horace Liveright. While the Urban League and its publication, *Opportunity*, were in many ways competition for the NAACP and *The Crisis*, theirs was a rivalry and not a battle to the death of the sort Du Bois had waged with Marcus Garvey. So Du Bois, James Weldon Johnson, and White were among the speakers encouraging the aggressive creation of works of art that truly expressed African-American life in all its complexity. It would be, according to Du Bois, "About Us; By Us; For Us; Near Us." Connections and ideas sparked out of the party, and two weeks later Du Bois's sixtieth birthday party assembled many of the same people for more of the same. A national tour by the black tenor Roland Hayes, whom White had met in London in 1921, added to the mix. Suddenly Harlem was the place to be.

Although *Fire in the Flint* was scheduled for publication in September, news of the Knopfs picking up the book had brought White congratulations from the likes of Eugene O'Neill, Carl Van Doren, and Konrad Bercovici, a free-spirited writer described in *Time* magazine as "one of these walrus-mustached foreigners who give a touch of the exotic to the reaches of the Hotel Algonquin, Manhattan." Now White was everywhere: raising a subscription to help the perennially destitute Claude McKay; sending a parcel of Countee Cullen's poetry to Van Doren at the *Century* magazine and setting up meetings for the young poet with Horace Liveright; even acting in a production of *Salome* at the Ethiopian Art Theatre at the 135th Street library. After so many years feeding stories to the press, White was not just well connected, he knew how to use his connections to start a buzz about his coming book. With Mencken he schemed to send copies to the most unfavorable Southern editors and newspapers possible in hopes of stirring up incendiary reviews that would only sell more copies. He canvassed friends across the country to solicit their thoughts about the book's chances in their areas, and made use of his ties in the wide-flung insurance industry. He drew up long lists of possible blurbs, and to help ensure good press he angled with friends and acquaintances for reviews, unmindful or uninterested in charges of logrolling.

Of course, kindly reviews of each other's books by friends is a practice that will likely continue as long as there are books to sell. But White's use of the NAACP to sell copies has occasioned questions about his ethics. In April 1924 White suggested that Knopf print a solicitation piece for use at the NAACP conference, of a sort that was displayed for other publications. The publisher did create a piece that boasted a blurb from James Weldon Johnson recommending that black readers buy a copy of White's book for themselves and "one for some white person." But White's suggestion that branch offices sell the book on his behalf seemed to some in the organization to cross a line. On the other hand, field secretary William Pickens, who would in time become one of White's greatest detractors, was explicit in a memo to White with his thoughts as to how to reach black book buyers, including the suggestion, "Whenever you speak in meeting, book can be sold after meeting, without interference with the interests of the meeting." When discussing a list of black bookstores, Pickens wrote, "We ought to have a list of this sort. Let's compile one." Clearly White was not alone in connecting the cause of the NAACP with the sales of *Fire in the Flint*. While his efforts to advance his book's fortunes through the organization could be seen as heavy-handed and obvious, little of it would raise an eyebrow today. In a marketing sense, he was ahead of his time.

The book did cause a splash, if not a rush on bookstores. Although it went into three printings between its publication in early September and Thanksgiving of 1924, sales apparently never broke ten thousand copies. Yet all of White's prepublication preparation paid off in notoriety. The vast majority of Southern papers reacted with the venom he'd hoped for, while most Northern reviewers forgave the book's workmanlike quality, stressing instead its raw depiction of a side of itself America would rather not see. When the book was published in England the next year, some British reviewers even flattered White with comparisons to *Uncle Tom's Cabin* for its groundbreaking importance. White's friend Bercovici saw how it would open doors to a flood of African-American writing, but Joel Spingarn delivered the finest gift, a quote from Sinclair Lewis, then at the peak of his success with *Babbitt* just out in 1922 and *Arrowsmith* on its way the next year. "It seems probable to me," Lewis blurbed, "that 'The Fire in the Flint' and 'A Passage to India' will prove much the most important books of this autumn . . . splendidly courageous, rather terrifying, and of the highest significance."

Mencken, Clement Wood, and Stribling, among others, all had their two cents for White. Wood made no bones about rating himself the better writer, and Stribling quibbled about word choice and a lack of humor, criticism that finally rubbed White the wrong way. "My dear Stribling," he responded, "why in the name of God must every story about the Negro drag in humor, real or alleged, by the scruff of the neck?" White could use every bit of advice he could get from these men, and much of what they offered was valid, but when Stribling questioned White's objectivity, it smacked of stung white pride hiding behind writing lessons. Lewis also had counsel, but unlike these lesser writers he understood what drove White, and he wasn't afraid of it. Although he repeated the general concern about being "more just to his 'villains,'" Lewis advised White to do so "not so much for any abstract justice but in order more successfully to attack them." Lewis and White would go on to a long friendship, with White later arranging for McKay to meet Lewis in Paris.

When White had sat down at the typewriter at Mary White Ovington's house, he'd had no fantasy of a writer's life. He and Dorothy West, the "kid" of the Harlem Renaissance who would go on to write *The Wedding*, had dabbled on a children's book called *Chocolate Child*, whose plot perhaps resembled too closely that of *Hazel*, by Ovington; and he'd written articles for national magazines. But all this attention for this book, these reviews heralding a new young writer, the guidance from well-known authors, seemed to change White's light attitude toward his fiction. What was once merely a sideline to his NAACP work, another thread in a rich life, became increasingly the design. Bumptiously he pursued tardy reviewers, and for those publications that hadn't yet assigned the book he suggested Eugene O'Neill, Dreiser, or Booth Tarkington as worthy critics. Egged on by Bercovici and O'Neill, he worked on a stage adaptation of the novel for Paul Robeson even as he started his next, *Flight*.

*

For all his good reviews and notoriety, though, what lifted White to the next social stratum was a new friend who would later be the source of many of the worst things ever said about him. In late August 1924, Bercovici mentioned to White that his friend Carl Van Vechten had read galleys of the book and, like him, felt it needed to be a play. The next day Van Vechten sent White a note, and the two met for a long chat in Van Vechten's apartment. White made quite an impression. As Van Vechten wrote to his friend, Edna Kenton, "He speaks

An operator like White, critic and man-about-town Carl Van Vechten would always maintain a connection to him even after their friendship soured. *(Library of Congress)*

French and talks about Debussy and Marcel Proust in an off-hand way. An entirely new kind of Negro to me. I shall, I hope, see something of these cultured circles."

Their first two hours together belong on any list of Harlem Renaissance landmarks, because Carl Van Vechten was the man who introduced Harlem to the white world through his articles in *Vanity Fair*, and it was Walter White who over the next two years introduced Van Vechten to Harlem. As steep as White's social learning curve was right now, so was Van Vechten's, with some fairly basic topics in the curriculum. "I am causing to have sent to you soon a novel," he wrote to a friend after his meeting with White, "*The Fire in the Flint*, written by a Nigger."

And yet for that, Van Vechten was a sincere student. His greatest talent was to be found not in his minor novels but in his ability to spot talent in others. Tall, bucktoothed, and gay (yet married—most of the time happily so, it seems—to the gaminlike Fania Marianoff), he started as a drama and music critic, then soon wove his tastes and enthusiasms into a glittering web of artist friends that reached around the globe and included Gertrude Stein, Dreiser, and Wallace Stevens. Like White, he was a medium through which current passed. But if White was a live wire, Van Vechten, campy before the term came into popular use, was an unctuous gel that spread a glow. Mirror images, between them the two men knew everyone worth knowing, and they immediately set about trading connections.

Socially, Walter and Gladys now found themselves above the clouds. Sweet Auburn must have seemed very far away. In October, Van Vechten's actress friend Marie Doro hosted a swank party in their honor, and a week later they were sitting with the Knopfs, Van Vechten, and Miguel Covarrubias, whose drawings of the Harlem Renaissance in *Vanity Fair* would be some of its most lasting images, as George Gershwin tried out some of his new compositions. Into the new year the Whites returned the favor, putting Van Vechten together with James Weldon Johnson, with whom he would remain lifelong friends, Paul Robeson, and other Harlem luminaries, and securing him invitations to the Riverdale mansion of A'Leila Walker, heiress to the Walker hair-products fortune and unquestioned social apex of Harlem. All the parties were avowedly, loudly, publicly interracial in a way that may seem forced today but was a courageous statement at a time when thousands of Klansmen paraded through the streets of Washington, D.C.

Thirty-one as the year ended, White had a finger in every socket and now, meeting new and fabulous people at every turn, he entertained the first serious offer to leave the NAACP. That spring he had pulled out all the stops for his friend Roland Hayes, arranging meetings and putting many of his influential contacts at Hayes's concerts. With White's personality, his connections, and his knack for publicity, it made sense that Hayes would ask him to become his manager. Gladys thought it was a good fit, but James Weldon Johnson shot it down. "Mr. Johnson doesn't welcome the idea of my leaving," White wrote Hayes, closing the matter. Gladys would have to be happy with a new piano while Walter, perhaps as a reminder of how he'd gotten to this place, was sent to Nashville just days before Christmas to investigate the lynching of a black teenager.

*

In 1925 White's whirl of the arts, society, and black advocacy went into overdrive. Now the grizzled veteran, he offered advice, entrees, and favorable reviews to Langston Hughes and Rudolph Fisher. Publishing houses, including the newly started Viking Press, tried to hire him as a talent scout, unleashing him on every writer he knew to get their manuscripts in shape, even as he continued work on *Flight*. Not only did he convince Paul Robeson to quit the law in favor of theater that year, but he worked a deal with Victor Talking Machines to record the great singer. He lent editorial help to Claude McKay on the early drafts of *Home to Harlem*, was a founding member of Du Bois's theatrical group, the Krigwa Players, and petitioned Carl Sandburg at the *Chicago Daily News* on behalf of Countee Cullen.

By May he was officially "no longer doing field work" for the NAACP, but a new case would consume him from September through the spring of 1926 and reveal the gap quietly widening between White and the people for whom he advocated. That August, Dr. Ossian Sweet, an African-American physician, moved his wife and baby daughter into a house in a marginal white neighborhood in Detroit. After weeks of brewing trouble throughout the city, a white mob attacked the house on the night of September 9. Sweet, his two brothers, and some friends who had gathered inside shot at the whites advancing onto the property, leaving one man dead and another injured. Sweet and the others were arrested, and a local defense team was assembled. The Detroit NAACP branch called the national office for help. In the wake of the anti-lynching campaign, one of Johnson's targets was housing segregation, and the Sweets, good representatives of the Talented Tenth, looked like perfect people to hang a case on. At the same time the organization was applying to the Garland Fund, a huge foundation built from the largesse of a young heir named Charles Garland, for money to seed its own legal defense fund. This would allow the NAACP to have its own lawyers on staff rather than being caught up in local politics, and to direct its own agenda of legal precedent, structural changes that would soon reveal a profound importance. Johnson accepted the case.

As he had in Elaine and Chicago, Walter White went to Detroit and took over the show. Only this was no longer the tricky young man fresh out of the South who wove tales of fooling Mr. Charlie. Much had changed since those daredevil years; now one was more likely to find White in a tuxedo, martini in hand, than in a church basement. His interest in blending into the landscape and reading the situation was minimal.

After meeting with Judge Ira Jayne, a member of the NAACP executive board, he decided that a white lawyer would best serve the Sweets' interests by appealing to moderate whites in this Northern city, something the defense team as it was currently assembled couldn't do. Inexperienced at best, unsavory at worst, the local black lawyers in place were not up to what the NAACP considered its standards. And White, not actually a lawyer, could also complicate matters with his own ad hoc legal opinions. A small civil war resulted as Detroit's black community reacted angrily to the top-down approach. When White refused to pay the full settlement the black lawyers wanted, the publicity grew even worse. Other competing defense funds were started until the Sweets finally ceded complete control to the NAACP and Johnson contacted Clarence Darrow. Famous for his defense of the spree killers Leopold and Loeb and his role in the Scopes Monkey Trial, Darrow took on the case and saw it through to victory. Not surprisingly, White chummed up with the great lawyer, who was bemused by White's racial ambiguity.

Although the Sweet case went down as a win, it dented White's reputation. He may have scored against white injustice, but he'd operated without the full support of the local black community. While placing the precedent of the case above local niceties had seemed farsighted in Elaine, in Detroit it had turned into a conflict of class. Unlike the besieged community in rural Arkansas, African Americans in Detroit were not impressed by White's name-dropping.

White was also simply doing too much. In the midst of the Sweet case he was still fund-raising, setting up the national convention, and handling other administrative duties—and too much of it was not being done especially well. The Sweet case succeeded because of the power of his position and the NAACP rather than a solid reading of the situation or a shrewd handling of its details. The sort of expedience that allowed White to survive as a small thing darting among giants exposed his shortcomings when writ large. Aside from Darrow's friendship and the general glory of another public victory, White took comfort in the salons of Harlem, where people still raised champagne toasts in his honor. But the reception to two books in 1926, his own *Flight*, and *Nigger Heaven* by his friend Van Vechten, made it clear how perilous the social heights could be for the inexperienced or overly ambitious.

White had delivered the manuscript of *Flight* to Blanche Knopf in September 1925, confident that he had matured as a novelist, and in some ways he had. A story of passing, *Flight* follows light-skinned Mimi Daquin and her parents out of New Orleans to Atlanta. Her father Jean sells insurance for a company modeled on Atlanta Life, and Mimi grows up traveling in the same elite circles as White. When a romance with the owner's son, Carl, results in pregnancy, instead of having an abortion Mimi moves to Philadelphia with her son, Petit Jean. But life is so hard that she must put the boy up for adoption and move in with an aunt in Harlem. While there, a gossip item exposing her past runs in a Harlem paper, so Mimi, disgusted by her race, begins a new life passing as a white seamstress. Quick with a needle, she works her way up at a dressmaker's shop until she accompanies her employer to Paris. Her new life is rewarding but dry, and after marrying a white man who is a closet racist, she is awakened at a party by a discussion with a Chinese man who talks about the painful legacy of the white race in history. Soon after, Mimi attends a concert at Carnegie Hall by a black singer in the heroic Hayes/Robeson mode, which inspires her to leave her husband, find her son, and resume her life as an African American.

Once again White set about banging his drum in the spring of 1926, floating sales deals with NAACP branch offices, roping in blurbs, and pitching the novel as a movie to Oscar Michaeux and others. His friends, including Sinclair Lewis, had good things to say, appreciating if not the book itself then how far he'd come as a craftsman. Press reviews were at best mixed. With passing already a common theme in Harlem Renaissance literature, the book lacked the shock value of *Fire in the Flint*.

While *Flight* is somewhat better written than White's first novel, boasting a few genuinely lovely passages, calling it mediocre would be generous. That he sincerely accepted the criticisms of *Fire in the Flint* shows: characters are more complex, and overall one isn't repeatedly hit over the head with a message. Still, it's a stodgy book, fussier than it is evocative. Dull Mimi, though more fully realized than Kenneth Harper, feels limp no matter what she does, and the tone points up the discord between White's oral telling of his exploits and the stories he will write later. White, the voluble, entertaining talker, commanded attention wherever he went; yet his fiction lacks any direct contact with the reader, feeling instead as if it had been written to earn approval rather than because, like the best novels, its truth simply had to be said.

Nettled, White alternated between puffing the good reviews and firing back at his critics. In his defense he never indulged in *schadenfreude*. There's little other than praise and encouragement in his letters, no cackling at bad reviews or poor sales. Some of that response may come from the relative shallows of White's artistic depth, but he sincerely understood that a rising tide lifted all boats. His self-importance was not at the expense of others, and he regularly extended himself even to unknowns who sent him unsolicited pages at the NAACP. So when he reacted with public petulance to a negative review in *Opportunity*, it turned the more self-possessed heads of Johnson and the Spingarns. After supporting so many artists with connections and reviews and money, he could not stand—or felt he should have been immune from—the open intellectual forum he had helped create. Irate, he demanded that Charles Johnson run a response by Nella Larsen, who essentially put her name to a rejoinder that her friend penned himself. When Johnson let the reviewer respond to Larsen, White couldn't hold back. He shot off a sniping retort, rich with phrases such as "It is beginning to become apparent that hereafter I must write two versions of any book I want understood—one of them designed for readers of normal intelligence or better; the other supplied with maps, charts, graphs and pictures and written in words of not more than two syllables."

Every novelist has had this thought, yet only the most foolish write it down, let alone demand that it be published. White may have intended to be patronizing, but instead he appeared to be publicly melting down along with his novel, under exactly the sort of serious critical scrutiny he aspired to. The bitterness of his reaction may also have had something to do with the response to his heroine Mimi Daquin, who is built—much more than Kenneth Harper—out of White's experiences and thoughts. In a letter to a board member, White wrote, "In telling of Mimi, I revealed, I now realize, a great deal more of myself than I knew at the time of writing." Rejection of her as a credible character went directly at White himself.

The unsatisfying publication of *Flight* turned into a firestorm when White's friend Van Vechten whipped up a frothy novel about Harlem society called *Nigger Heaven*, published by Knopf. Reaction uptown was fast, hot, and nearly unanimous in its condemnation. To most, this white visitor introduced by White had used his free passage through Harlem parlors and parties to portray them in a bad light. Johnson and White, though, stood strongly at Van Vechten's side, defending him against even Du Bois, who called the book a "blow to the face." White countered, "It ought to be welcomed by African Americans for raising whites' awareness of the race issue"—each word opening the gap between himself and everyday black America just a little wider. As more strident and intellectually demanding writers such as Zora Neale Hurston and Wallace Thurman and Langston Hughes—all of whom were quite obviously black—explored subjects such as politics, sexuality, and folklore, or traveled to the Soviet Union and debated the economic conditions of poor blacks, the fair-skinned White appeared to be in the thrall of a white dilettante.

*

If he registered this decline in his stock, White didn't show it, remaining devoted to the potential of Harlem. In the fall of 1926 he formed a trading corporation with Nella Larsen's husband Elmer Imes, Paul Robeson, and Dr. Louis T. Wright. When Van Vechten mentioned opening a bookstore in Harlem, White took the idea and ran with it, suggesting a black book-of-the-month club. Van Vechten, though, backed out. Harlem, specifically 90 Edgecombe, was also about to get a new resident. Just after finishing a part in the short run of the opera *Deep River*, starring Julius Bledsoe, Gladys discovered she was pregnant again.

According to his second wife, Poppy Cannon, White later confessed that it was around this time that his marriage to Gladys soured. There are obvious reasons—the stress of their lifestyle; their incompatibility, obvious to everyone but them; the vanity and perfectionism they both shared. Yet there's still a mystery here that may relate to the pregnancy and the opera. Some have implied that White, a most controlling spouse and father, insisted on a second child, possibly to keep Gladys from taking any more theater work that would allow her to edge into his spotlight. On the other hand, given White's tepid embrace of the boy who would be born the next year, it may be that she had insisted on the child.

Whatever the cause, the marriage was in trouble when, in late October, White left his pregnant wife and young daughter for Aiken, South Carolina, and one of his final two personal investigations. In the summer of 1925, police in Aiken had surrounded the Lowman family home on the pretext that they were moonshiners. As the family retreated inside, the sheriff hit one of the teenaged children. Mrs. Lowman then attacked the sheriff with an axe and was shot. The ensuing gun battle left the sheriff dead and all surviving members of the Lowman family in jail. Despite proof that the evidence presented for the initial police search had been planted, the three children were all found guilty, two of them sentenced to death and one to life in prison. A successful appeal resulted in a retrial in October 1926, but when the eventual release of the three looked probable, a mob took them out of prison and lynched them.

The account White writes of this investigation a few years later is misleading in an important way. As he tells it in "I Investigate Lynchings," he went down to Aiken for the *New York World*. This much is true. He then claims that he meets a lawyer who knows the real story. The lawyer takes him out to a shack in the middle of nowhere to see a man who greets White and then disappears. A few tense moments later, a door opens and out comes someone in full Klan garb. White starts, but then the hood comes off and it's the owner of the shack, who turns out to be the local kleagle, ready now to tell all about the Klan-infested town.

In fact, both the lawyer and the Klansman had been in touch with the NAACP before White's visit. The meetings were prearranged and hardly the walk into the lion's den that White describes them as. Be that as it may, the Klansman, James Quinby, revealed how the Klan had infiltrated all levels of the town and ran the bootlegging business the Lowmans had been accused of running.

Whatever White's embellishment, the results of this investigation were significant. As soon as he left Aiken, he sent a six-page letter to South Carolina governor Thomas MacLeod which laid out all he had found, including a detailed list of conspirators and Klan control that lapped onto the door of the governor's office, and giving him forty-eight hours to act before White released it all to the press. When MacLeod failed to pursue the case, White passed all he learned to the *New York World*, which sent a star reporter to investigate and keep the pressure on. Public opinion both inside the borders of South Carolina and out ran heavily against the lynchers and the state government, which in some cases were associated. Although the murderers were never arrested, the idea of lynching as an acceptable substitute for constitutional justice had become publicly repellent. Lynchings would continue, with a serious rise during the depression, but no longer with the silent sanction of American society.

Before he left for South Carolina, though, White had made a profound decision: if he wasn't ready to change his personal life, he was ready to leave the NAACP. At some point during the process of writing *Flight*, he had deluded himself into believing that his true calling was not with the NAACP but as a writer, in particular a novelist. His artistic friends did not have to contend with the likes of office manager Richetta Randolph, the cranky Detroit branch office, or Klansmen, and the money they made looked good too. (In May 1925 White had tried desperately to interest Cecil B. DeMille in a screen adaptation of *Fire in the Flint*, which he, of course, intended to write.) White's nonfiction was now regularly published in national magazines and newspapers, and he had a column in the *Pittsburgh Courier*, one of the country's leading black newspapers. Nor was his take on fiction wrongheaded. In a series for *The Crisis* about black literature, he steered clear of championing either sensational tales of seedy Harlem life or Du Bois's vision of art as propaganda. Instead, he argued, there was no right kind of black literature nor one right way of writing it. If black writers told honest, compelling stories, and did so with skill, they would be heard. White did not see that he lacked the talent to realize his own good advice.

Thus in October 1926, while he investigated Aiken, White secretly submitted his application to the Guggenheim Foundation for a three-year grant to pursue a writing career. The board of the NAACP was not pleased when it heard word of this, and in November Joel Spingarn called White in for an audience to explain why he was walking away from what he'd assumed was White's "lifework." Spingarn later described a puzzling and disconcerting scene in which he asked White if he believed that darker-skinned blacks were less developed than fair-skinned ones. After much protest, White "admitted that he had virtually never met a pure Negro whom he really could trust, that he didn't believe it was in them, that they were inferior, infinitely inferior now, whatever they might possibly become in future. So there's the conflict," Spingarn continued, "—nine-tenths white loathing the one-tenth black, one-tenth black hating the nine-tenths white. The passionate pro-Negro loyalty is a conflict, a whirlpool—and a mask."

Even historian Kenneth Janken, who takes a dim view of White's motives under most circumstances, finds this story far-fetched, at best a description of White telling the paternalist Spingarn what he wanted to hear to guarantee a letter of recommendation for the Guggenheim. Yet White's own comments about his fraternity and the house on Houston Street, the family's rude treatment on the streetcars of Atlanta, point to a bitterness toward darker-skinned blacks that, as he assumed he was nearing the start of a new career, may have found voice in Spingarn's sitting room.

White was awarded a Guggenheim in March 1927, but it was not the intellectual coronation he'd hoped for. Although his plan had been to move Gladys and the children to France for three years and work on a sprawling family saga, his fellowship provided only one year. Rather than making a clean break with the NAACP, White took a sabbatical, to start in July.

With Gladys eight months pregnant and plans in full swing for their departure, White was called away for his last personal investigation, a May 1927 journey through the Mississippi Delta, where millions of acres had been devastated and hundreds of thousands of people displaced by the great flood of that year, a disaster comparable to Hurricane Katrina of 2005. Evidence mounted amid the mismanaged federal relief program that thousands of African-American refugees, at first sent out of stricken areas, were now being held against their will in work camps. White went to the Delta to investigate the effectiveness of the relief effort and these reports of peonage, appealing to the *New York Times* for credentials. When the *Times* refused, White went forward on his own, finding ample evidence of ill treatment. Sudden illness forced him back to New York after a week, but even with the distraction of a son born on June 8 and a European move in a month, White attacked those responsible with the usual passion. Sending his findings to Commerce Secretary Herbert Hoover, he also worked his publicity channels, including a piece in *The Nation* called "The Negro and the Flood."

Although he was a Republican, which for much of black America still meant the party of Lincoln, Hoover offered no help and instead did everything he could to defend himself and the Red Cross. "White is literally the nigger in the woodpile," wrote one of Hoover's staffers, "and if anything can be done to placate or squelch him I think there will be no more trouble." Both the Urban League and Tuskegee came out in support of Hoover, leaving White and the NAACP as the only voices for destitute blacks in the Mississippi Delta and against the unchecked power of white America to reduce African Americans to a state of virtual slavery when it so chose.

*

As the White family boarded the *Carmania* for Le Havre on July 23, 1927, they may well have felt an invisible hand pushing them across the ocean. Walter and Gladys had developed a reputation for high-handedness and for dropping the names of fancy white friends such as Darrow and Van Vechten while many neighbors in Harlem rolled their eyes. The desire to have his rightful place at the best tables continued to distance White from those who just wanted their daily bread. And then, after publicly going to the mat for Van Vechten, White lost him as a friend. Although the reasons were never stated by either, and White, ever the gentleman, afterward never referred to Van Vechten with anything less than kindness, a clumsy bit of social dishonesty on White's part around the naming of their son seems to have brought about the split. At some point during Gladys's pregnancy, apparently Clarence Darrow had said he'd like the child named after him. Calling the boy Carl killed a few birds with one stone—the Whites could not only tell Darrow that he was the boy's namesake, but they also led Van Vechten to believe the same, as well as a doctor friend in Chicago, Carl Roberts. (White obviously had an affinity for the name Carl; he'd given the name to Mimi Daquin's feckless lover Carl Hunter in *Flight*.)

Naming his son after the two prominent white men he famously courted and, in Van Vechten's case, defended, did not go down well uptown. Nella Larsen, who herself was of mixed race and more distracted with the fact than White ever was, appears to be the one who instigated the final rupture with Van Vechten. Larsen and Van Vechten had become close, and when he told her about the silver Tiffany's cup he'd just had engraved for the baby, Larsen spilled the rumors about Carl's multiple namesakes. Clearly the friendship between White and Larsen had become tangled as well; he had done much for her and would in the future, and she had willingly, if unwisely, helped him take on *Opportunity* magazine. But at this point at least, she had it out for him. "They intend to look you up," she wrote her friend Dorothy Peterson in Paris, "and you have my deepest sympathy."

White's sense of expedience, his fast talking, had cost him dearly. Wounded, Van Vechten left only unkind words about the man who'd not just introduced him to the source of his greatest fame but stood by him when he made questionable use of it. In the Columbia University Oral History Research Office Collection, Van Vechten says that in 1923 White worked in a "minor capacity" in the NAACP and that he was "a hustler," "a show-off," and "a blowhard." "I was never completely sold on Walter," he claims. "I mean, he always struck me as not as good a thing as the NAACP seemed to think he was." He goes on to say that "Walter knew after a while that I was no particular use to him and he was less use to me too as far as that goes." Like his claim that Walter was a minor player in the NAACP in 1923, the same year White firmed his power base with the Elaine case, this is bitchier than it is true. Van Vechten also, in antebellum fashion, took umbrage at Walter's penchant for immediately entering on a first-name basis, saying it embarrassed other blacks who allegedly couldn't do so themselves. Not only did he miss the signifying aspect of the act, but Van Vechten, who closed letters with lines such as "151 mulatto gals with red hair and blue silk panties to you," was, as seen in the letter quoted earlier, able as late as 1924 to refer to White as "a Nigger" behind his back, calling into question his expertise on the mind of black America. While they would politely communicate in the years to come, the mirror had broken for each of them.

It's impossible to know how deeply this stung White. Although he was a loyal friend—Nella Larsen, for example, continued to run White down and yet continued to receive his help for the next decade—chummy and charming by all accounts, he was not a man of intimacies. None of his letters confess secret dreams or true opinions; they're all written for effect, a combination of his AU education, a salesman's hard shell, and the formal proprieties of the White family. Ultimately White was not concerned with profundities and emotion. He wanted to be known, and since his happiest moments were public, his private and family lives shrunk accordingly, to the detriment of his marriage and children. Such men and women may not make for moral heroes, but history books are filled with them.

*

After a night in Paris and a private performance by Isadora Duncan at his agent's home, the Whites headed south and settled ino a villa in Villefranche, near Nice. Gladys sent a photo of her son to Larsen, but on the back of the picture, instead of a name, she wrote "Brother." The embarrassing name situation had yet to be resolved, news that Nella glee-fully relayed. And Dorothy Peterson waved a knife of her own in a letter to Van Vechten: "Somehow or other I missed seeing your godson when he passed thru Paris. I think per-haps his father is passing for French or maybe French colonial or something like that." Unpleasant an image as that may be, it certainly fits with the White family ethos of not telling one's race unless asked, though Walter's soft Southern burr would have given him away to any Frenchman. Their neigh-bors in Villefranche eventually dubbed Carl *le petit pigeon*, which Walter and Gladys jumped on. They now called him Pidge; legally he would eventually become Walter Carl Dar-row White and later, bitterly, just Carl Darrow.

It would be nice to call these months an idyll, but as usu-al Walter was at the typewriter every day. What the sun of the south of France inspired though, instead of a novel, was *Rope and Faggot: A Biography of Judge Lynch*, a sociologi-cal investigation of lynching in America. *Rope and Faggot* takes apart Southern society and isolates the elements that

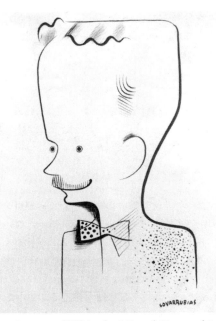

A caricature of White by Miguel Covarrubias, a Mexican artist whose drawings of the Harlem Renaissance appeared in *Vanity Fair* and the *New Yorker*. *(Yale Collection of American Literature, Beinecke Rare Book and Manuscript Library)*

make heinous torture and murder possible, eliminating the one cause—black sexuality—that most white Americans believed was at the root of lynching. Although Ida Wells-Barnett had written on lynching earlier and had developed some of the ideas, especially regarding sexuality as it affects racial violence, White does not mention her in the book. (Today she receives more than her share of the credit in the battle against lynching, compared to the all but forgotten White, so her revenge on him for any uncredited borrowings seems complete.) Rather than sex crimes committed by black men against white women, White shows that main-

taining white economic power was lynching's true motivation. It is a driving statement of the NAACP anti-lynching
campaign, cleanly written and with a more mature passion
than White displayed in *Fire in the Flint*. Historians generally agree with his conclusions, but the fact that he arrived
at them anecdotally rather than through statistical studies
keeps *Rope and Faggot* from the landmark status given to
the works of Du Bois and E. Franklin Frazier. Some academ-
ics fault it for not examining philosophies of violence and
other such abstruse topics, a quality that in fact makes it a
more relevant and readable book.

In his autobiography White claims that rather than getting away from it all in France, he felt drawn that much
closer to the problem of lynching, and so he found that he
couldn't concentrate on the novel. Given that there were
sixteen lynchings in the United States in 1927 and eleven
in 1928, compared to fifty-seven in 1922 and thirty in 1926,
this doesn't seem entirely honest.

He finished *Rope and Faggot* in January 1928. By now
tight funds had driven the Whites to a flat in Avignon, where
he began a new novel, this one about a boxer—not the intended family saga. The next year he happily reported his
progress to Blanche Knopf, but then the subject disappears,
never discussed again and only recently rediscovered among
White's papers in the Schomburg Collection, on the site of
Ernestine Rose's 135th Street branch of the New York Public Library. *Rope and Faggot* is an intelligent, convincing
book, but it lacks the literary cachet of a novel, and it wasn't
what he had surely told everyone within earshot that he
was leaving America to do. What likely dawned on White
during his French sojourn was the disappointing truth that
despite his acquaintance with Ford Maddox Ford and Som-
erset Maugham, he would never join the ranks of America's
greatest novelists. Blithe as he is about this failure in *A Man*

Called White, it was a very public embarrassment all the same, and he would continue to bristle defensively when he felt his work slighted, even, in 1929, refusing a bronze award from the prestigious Harmon Foundation for *Rope and Faggot* because he felt he deserved the gold. The white skies of the Riviera and the blank paper in his typewriter had made it clear that, like his former partner in crime Van Vechten, he was a better salesman than artist. In years to come he would noodle with movie scripts and plays, create controversies in Hollywood, and shoot off snarky criticisms to performers who didn't reach his standards, but White's misguided fling as a full-time artist had come to an end. A letter in March 1928 brought him back early to the United States for a new job offer, one that was not with the NAACP.

CHAPTER FIVE

Conflict, Control, and the Making of Mr. NAACP

⌘ When not terrorized or otherwise kept from the polls, African Americans had voted as a virtual bloc for Republican candidates from the end of the Civil War. The choice had been easy, if not always deeply considered: a Republican president had ended slavery, a Republican administration had given blacks participation in American life. The Democrats, meanwhile, would go to any extreme to maintain their Southern fortress. Over the years the Republican party took increasing advantage of this loyalty, assuming black votes and offering nothing in return, even as GOP candidates began to walk and talk like Southern Democrats, promoting segregation and disfranchisement in order to compete for votes. With the likely Republican candidate for president Herbert Hoover, who had proved himself no friend of black America during the 1927 floods, and former New York governor Al Smith running on the Democratic ticket, many African Americans were reconsidering their traditional link to the Grand Old Party as the 1928 election approached.

The telegram White received in Avignon came from Charles Studin, NAACP board member, one of the premier hosts of the Harlem Renaissance, and by day Arthur Spingarn's law partner. Seeing the opportunity offered by millions of disaffected black Republicans, the Smith campaign

was looking for an African American with charisma and political acumen to lead a concerted drive for black votes—a
perfect fit for Walter White, thought Studin. Within days
White was on a boat back to New York. In many ways this
job answered all his questions. With his literary career over,
here was a new path, independent yet reassuringly close to
the one he'd been on at the NAACP, and pointing directly to
power. If Smith were to win the White House with his help,
White would become a major player in the administration.
The risks, though, were significant. Since the NAACP was
avowedly nonpartisan, he would have to quit to join up with
Smith, leaving no safety net under himself and his family.
For all his flamboyance, White hadn't lost the need for security he'd had in 1917, when he told Roy Nash that he had his
life all planned out.

   White did not make the choice on his own; his presence
in the campaign was desired precisely because of his connection to the NAACP, and opinions there were divided. Tom
Watson and the Populists had taught black America a sour
lesson in betrayal, and so far the Democrats had shown little
cause for trust. The electoral calculus of the nation had not
changed since the writing of the Constitution—tribute still
had to be paid to the South if you meant to win the White
House—and the Democrats, many at the NAACP feared,
would sell out black America to get there.

   While White negotiated and his family went on sunning
in France, he wrote a solid diagnosis of how Smith could
benefit from the black vote. During the fight for the Dyer
Bill he'd learned more than just backslapping, and what he
lacked as a theoretician he more than made up for with raw
political expertise and will. White leaned toward the job as
the July convention approached, but as the assurances of the
Smith campaign for support of black interests grew weaker,
the risks increased. The power of the NAACP would be de-

stroyed within the black community if White and, by proxy, the group were taken in by empty Democratic promises. Nor did White, personal ambitions aside, want the position if Smith wasn't serious about civil rights. Finally White and Johnson sent Smith a statement to endorse, which would put him on record as supporting much of the NAACP platform. When Smith chose not to sign on for fear of scaring off Southern Democrats, White walked away with no apparent regrets. Although he helped the Smith campaign in minor ways that fall, he never came out in full support. Hoover won the presidency. In later years Smith admitted regret that he had not taken the stand White and Johnson had offered.

Back now from France, the White family moved into a new apartment at 409 Edgecombe Avenue, in the Sugar Hill section of Harlem. Everyone, it appeared, was mellowed or chastened by the experience abroad—"Gladys White is ever so much more charming since her return," wrote Nella Larsen to a friend. White, though, was not satisfied now with much in his life. A conversation he'd shared at one of Studin's parties with a chatty and quite married food writer named Poppy Cannon grew into flirty lunches. *Rope and Faggot* came out in the spring of 1929, but unlike his usual frenzy of activity, White handled the publication with more restraint, often appearing with Larsen, whose first novel *Passing* had also just been published. That rapprochement lasted only a few months, though. Once Dorothy Peterson leaked to Gladys the naming story that Nella had been telling everyone, the Whites cut her out of their social circle, at least for now.

White's greatest dissatisfaction, however, was at work, and the NAACP was now work for him. His fellowship over, his political dreams aborted, he took his seat at the same desk, in the same office, with the same title he'd left behind in July 1927, supposedly forever. At thirty-five he'd outgrown the role of right hand to James Weldon Johnson, who could still refer to him as his "executive helper" (or at least Du Bois claims he called him that). "White was not co-operating as usual," Du Bois reports Johnson saying to him. That springy willingness to chase after every issue was flagging. The job's toll on Johnson was high too, physically and psychologically, and whether he and White ever spoke about succession, or whether White simply began to carry less of the burden in order to speed the process—something Johnson's wife would suspect in later years—in September Johnson took a year's sabbatical. With a Rosenwald Fellowship he planned to write and to attend a conference in Japan. The board named Walter White acting secretary of the NAACP.

A month later, on October 24, Black Thursday brought the 1920s crashing to earth, sending waves of suffering and upheaval through the nation that would last a decade. Saving a shattered economy—and preserving democracy—would mean rewriting the rules of business and upsetting assumptions about class and power in America. For White and the NAACP, high adventure, book prizes, and gin would give way to infighting, survival, and the responsibility to guarantee blacks a place in the New Deal. At home, in Harlem, everywhere in America, the romance was over. White became a harder man, a pragmatist out of necessity, desire, and the limits of his mind as he navigated a cautious path through a nation in crisis. The buoyant enthusiasm that endeared him to so many became an obsession to keep control of the NAACP, and to keep the NAACP in control of a black agenda that spread beyond the boundaries of the old definitions of civil rights. Although his every shortcoming would be revealed in the struggle, White's personal politicking and loose alliance with the New Deal, as part of its "loyal opposition," would ultimately leave him at the top of an NAACP alive and moving forward, and contribute significantly to a new sense

of federal responsibility for the welfare of African Americans. By the time the Nazis rolled into Poland in 1939, the NAACP and White were welded to each other, both stronger than ever, and considered by many a part of the very power structure they claimed to challenge.

*

When Johnson left, the reins were not simply handed over to White. His relative youth and erratic sense of finances raised concerns among many NAACP executives, including Du Bois and the Spingarn brothers. The same man who counted his expense pennies in traveling salesman's diaries could also be wildly extravagant with gifts and rub the borders of ethical bounds by wheedling a scholarship he probably didn't need for his daughter Jane to attend the Ethical Culture School on New York's Upper West Side. To keep an eye on him, the board created a Committee on Administration, consisting of Ovington as chairman, the Spingarns, and Isadore Martin, president of the Philadelphia branch. Until 1935, weekly meetings with the COA provided a check on White's authority and excesses—but it must also share in the responsibility for some of his poor decisions. Over time it became an advantage for him, providing constant access to the powers, and placing him in the position of problem solver. When push came to shove during power struggles, the COA more often than not came down on the side of White. William Pickens and Robert Bagnall were made associate secretaries, just a notch below him.

Although Johnson had confidence in his protégé, he was also leaving him with a long-term plan for accomplishments the NAACP desperately needed—and, hopefully, the money for executing it. After the campaign for the Dyer Bill, the organization had for the most part defined broad areas of concern and waited for cases that would typify them. The result was a series of small victories and a drop in membership from ninety thousand in 1919 to twenty thousand in 1929. The new plan, developed by Johnson and the Committee on Negro Work within the Garland Fund, called for a series of legal challenges on a slate of issues, including unequal apportionment of school funds, residential segregation, and Jim Crow travel accommodations. Named the Margold Plan after Nathan Margold, the New York attorney who researched and plotted the strategy, it mapped a path through the American legal system that would lead, decades later, to an end to segregation. Roger Baldwin, the Garland Fund's president, doubted the NAACP could do it and preferred to work with an offshoot committee of the Communist party. The stakes were high—a grant of $100,000—and the importance of that amount of money was already clear when the NAACP filed its final application for the grant only two weeks after Black Thursday.

Guided and counseled into a corner, White accepted these limitations, but as soon as the opportunity presented itself for him to put his own stamp on the NAACP, he grabbed it, and again energized it in a way no one, not even Du Bois, could.

*

With the death of Supreme Court Justice Edward Sanford on March 21, 1930, President Hoover nominated as his replacement North Carolina Republican judge John J. Parker. At only forty-five years of age, Parker was relatively inexperienced, but he'd proven popular in a failed bid for governor of a state the Republicans were eager to wrest from the Democrats. Parker supported public education, women's suffrage, and other progressive policies, but within days of the nomination an NAACP operative found an interview Parker had given in 1920 in which he supported black disfranchisement. African Americans were, he had said, "a source of evil and danger" in American politics. White jumped on this with the same vigor he'd displayed in 1918, when he'd volunteered to go to Estill Springs. A telegram to Parker asking for an explanation went unanswered, so the next day White went on the offensive, directing all 177 branches to petition their senators to vote against the nominee, and gearing up the NAACP's publicity machinery for a campaign unlike anything since the Dyer Bill.

On April 5 White appeared before the Senate Judiciary Committee, the last witness in the Parker hearings. It was not his best performance. He admitted to Senator William Borah of Idaho that all the NAACP had against Parker was the quote, but White already understood that his testimony wouldn't swing the vote. Instead he continued to throw the full force of the NAACP at the senators likely to vote for Parker, sending staffers—all the way up to Du Bois—on the road, building the opposition. Out of his tuxedo and into a suit, White traveled to meetings in Chicago, Detroit, and Cleveland to deliver fiery speeches of the sort he used to give against lynching. At the same time he drummed up popular support, reaching out to Southern liberals, such as the Commission on Interracial Cooperation, religious groups, and organized labor, who had their own qualms about Parker, and kept the publicity effort in full battle mode, ready to react. When Parker supporters denied the judge had ever made the statement in question, the next day White had a copy of the article in which it appeared on the desk of every senator and in the hands of every Washington correspondent. Confident of his confirmation, Parker never mounted a counterattack. On May 7 the Senate rejected his nomination 41 to 39, with anywhere from ten to sixteen votes swayed by the NAACP's campaign. For the first time in American history, a Supreme Court nomination had been blocked by pressure from interest groups.

Even White's detractors admitted that he'd orchestrated a grand success at a crucial moment. The campaign, wrote Du Bois, had been "conducted with snap, determination, and intelligence never surpassed in Colored America and very seldom in white." "I never have seen the 'brothers' cooperating so superbly," White wrote to George Schuyler. "The NAACP had taken to slugging," said Roy Wilkins in admiration from Kansas City, where he edited the *Kansas City Call*. Once again the NAACP had united black America behind a cause, and White saw the potentially dramatic effect this could have beyond Parker. Notice had been given to both parties that black activism—specifically by the NAACP, which had also just been awarded the $100,000 pledge from the Garland Fund—could make a difference. Now, like a smart general, White pursued the retreating troops, vowing to defeat in the November midterm elections those senators who had voted for Parker.

Like the best of his work, White combined goals: driving the larger cause by encouraging more, and better organized, local efforts by branches against the Parker supporters. The value of the branches to him was in raising money for the headquarters. Until then, he wrote to a board member, the NAACP had been "a little too kindly in its methods of raising funds." Undemocratic as that sounds, it wasn't all that different from how headquarters at Standard Life must have viewed their salesmen out in the sticks. And it was the same top-down, corporate view of the NAACP structure that had existed since the days of the Talented Tenth.

Nor is it a surprising sentiment from someone whose experience of "mass action" to this point had been limited to lynch mobs, riots, and Communist revolution. Later in his life White was outspoken in his support of Gandhi and Indian nationalism, and certainly agreed with nonviolence as a concept. But in White's time the philosophical underpinnings that Dr. King built on in the fifties and sixties were only beginning to show signs of effectiveness—Britain would not grant India its independence until 1947. White was far from alone in being wary of mass action at a time when bottom-up change connoted violent upheaval more than personal empowerment.

More to the point was Reinhold Niebuhr's *Moral Man and Immoral Society*, published in 1932, an influential meditation on the complex and often oppositional relationship between the individual and society in questions of moral action. Like White, the well-known theologian was a socialist voter turned New Dealer, and his belief in a pragmatic gradualism paralleled White's working methods. "We have never had the opportunity," wrote Niebuhr, "—and probably never shall have—to choose between injustice and perfect equality, but only between injustice and a justice which moves toward equality and incorporates some of its values." In the wake of World War II, Niebuhr would create the intellectual setting for White's leadership of the NAACP and his final break with Du Bois. But here in the 1930s Niebuhr seemed to predict White's future: "No doubt every socialist leader who has succumbed to the temptation of prestige and power had an Achilles heel of personal vanity and ambition, which one would hope not to find in a leader of purer metal." Walter White, a mixture of class and color, identified his value in not being purely anything.

*

The fall of 1930 was one of White's peaks. White, Bagnall, Pickens, and the recently hired Daisy Lampkin stirred pots everywhere, with most of the attention coming down to two races—in Kansas, where Roy Wilkins helped direct efforts to defeat Henry Allen, and in Ohio, where Roscoe McCulloch ran against Democrat Robert Bulkley for an open Senate

seat. Many inside the NAACP were concerned about supporting a Democrat in a traditional Republican state, but White
believed in Bulkley and waded into an ugly race filled with
dirty tricks that climaxed at a rally just before election day.
As White took the podium, he called up a local McCulloch
supporter who had infiltrated the meeting, then produced a
transcript of a speech this Reverend Olden had just given.
White read it aloud, mocking Olden all the way and driving
the crowd into a pitch—a pure display of the verbal one-
upmanship he'd mastered on the anti-lynching trail. As a
witness described the scene to Janken, "The crowd was wild
to touch him, to speak to him, to do homage to him." The
hall emptied, and the call went up, "WHAT'S THE MATTER
WITH WALTER WHITE. HE'S ALL RIGHT. WHO'S ALL RIGHT.
WALTER WHITE."

For someone with an ego the size of White's, this had to
be an overwhelming moment, adding to his own growing
sense of power. In July 1930, falling revenues for *The Crisis*
had forced Du Bois to ask the board to bring the magazine
under its financial control, and as part of the restructuring
White had secured a seat on the board, overseeing the titan
of black thought twenty-five years his senior. Marc Connelly
and the producers of the all-black Broadway show *The Green
Pastures* had asked White to approve their production, thus
acknowledging him as an important cultural arbiter. And as
the year closed, James Weldon Johnson announced that his
declining health and the offer of a prestigious professorship
at Fisk University had persuaded him to step away from the
pressures of the secretary's office. In March 1931 the board
named White, thirty-seven years old, permanent secretary.
The path to fame and power was now clear.

And White had changed. Living in a space between
races, until now he had stressed his blackness, but as his
contact with the white power structure increased, he posi-

tioned himself for its consumption. When he'd taken over as acting secretary in 1929, he had written up his investigations in magazine stories such as "I Investigate Lynchings," in the process turning them into shadows of what they'd once been in those church basements. Whereas any folktale about the Signifying Monkey or Anansi the Spider can be told in many different ways and remain the same story, relying on exactly that adaptability to stay fresh and alive, White had now created the "official" version, one version out of many possible versions committed to paper as if it were the only one. Sifting through the various written versions of his stories—whether or not he had a gun, or was sworn into a posse, and the like—it's vital to keep in mind what the scholar Henry Louis Gates, Jr., calls "the curious tension between the black vernacular and the literate white text, between the spoken and the written word, between the oral and the printed forms of literary discourse. . . ." The transmission of White's stories to white America (and greater fame) demanded they be written, but that took them out of the more fluid oral tradition and cast them as journalism. It preserved them forever but drained them of their vitality and forced an uncomfortable relation to the empirical facts that had never seemed quite as important when White was standing in front of a crowd in Memphis, explaining how he escaped a general store filled with murderous crackers.

While obviously African-American letters by the 1920s operated in the written word, the oral tradition had remained a living strain of expression and communication. Given the limited access of most of black America to the written word, the spoken word was probably the most effective way for White to enter himself and his stories into the mainstream of black thought. He'd grown up in the Fourth Ward, light skinned, but surely exposed to and participating in oral tradition. That White had made such masterful use of it seems not a desperate attempt at credibility but proof that he had operated comfortably within ordinary black cultural exchange, and was embraced for it.

But now the bon vivant, the trickster, was gone: "I found myself with less and less time for the theater, baseball, parties, writing, or any of the other diversions which had formerly lightened the load of problems and hard work," White wrote in his autobiography. His chameleon ability required a deep faith, a devotion to something essential, to transcend just a survival skill. Despite, or maybe because of, his family's connection to First Church, investigating lynchings brought White largely to disdain religion, blaming it in *Rope and Faggot* for "decades of cruelty, greed, and savagery almost beyond belief." He'd tried art but found at best a critic inside; hearth and home weren't the answer either: his marriage had failed. Professionally charming with the rest of the world, in his living room White was silent and distant, unable to relax; his family exhaled only when he walked out the door. Combined with Gladys's controlling nature and her own ability to freeze people out, Jane and Pidge now suffered through arid childhoods of high-pressure dinner table discussions, unreasonable expectations, and a father who, despite his overwhelming presence, became emotionally absent. Posed photographs show Carlo blank-faced, a little stunned by it all, and Jane keeping her own unhappy counsel, looking unsure about whom she's most angry with.

With God, art, and family left wanting, White now put his faith in the one thing he cared about most: himself. And since he defined blackness as himself, his cause became for him inseparable from his personal interests. Where a martyr offers his life for his beliefs, White merged his identity with his genuine and profound devotion to civil rights. "Mr. NAACP," as he would come to be called, had been born.

*

Du Bois was aghast at White's ascension. Seeing this coming, he, along with Pickens and a number of other senior-level staffers, had in January cajoled the board for a change in the bylaws that would limit White's authority over them. A jolly and engaging companion outside, Mr. NAACP had so far proved himself to be a domineering, almost suffocating, manager at the new office at 69 Fifth Avenue. "I note that there has been some laxity in registering on the time clock hours of arrival and departure at the office. In a few instances these omissions are glaring," read one of his staff memos, as stiff and scratchy as his father's horsehair kneelers. "Please see that this rule is rigidly adhered to." Insecure more about his control over the organization than about the color of his skin, White transformed his father's simple belief that God was in the details into grueling micromanagement. He threw in a dose of Heman Perry's martinet style to boot. He observed how many times staffers went to the bathroom, allowed no personal phone calls. "There was none of the camaraderie of a newspaper office, no joking, wisecracks, or kidding," wrote Roy Wilkins, who came as assistant secretary that year, recruited by Du Bois as a foil to White. White was turning the think tank, the nursery of ideas that Du Bois was accustomed to, into a corporation, and not a particularly enlightened one when it came to personnel policy. After all, Number 6 of the Life Insurance Temperament is the "Tendency to want to dominate those with whom you come in contact." "His attitude and actions," said Du Bois, "were unbearable."

Run-ins with Pickens and publicity director Herbert Seligman only raised the temperature. The atmosphere was poisonous. "The pall of office politics and intrigue was

W. E. B. Du Bois, the towering black intellectual. Through the early 1930s he and White
battled for control of the NAACP. *(Library of
Congress)*

thicker than smog in Los Angeles," Wilkins reported. But
Du Bois's concerns for the staff hid—poorly—his own political bruises. The perilous state of *The Crisis* meant a running
in-house battle for funds, pitting White and Du Bois in a
constant competition that became philosophical and personal. "Johnson's wife thought Walter had pushed her husband out, and Walter had yet to establish his own authority
around the shop," wrote Wilkins who, at least as much an
opportunist as White if a bit more grounded, signed on for
the coup. "Pickens, Bagnall, and Dr. Du Bois each believed
he would have made a better secretary than Walter, and Dr.
Du Bois was leading a campaign to topple him."

White finally had the tiller in his hand, but a storm was
about to hit.

*

A few weeks after White's coronation, nine black vagrants—
teenagers, really—were arrested after a fight with a group of
white boys as their freight train passed through Alabama.
Two white girls were with the blacks at the time. Rather
than suffer the repercussions of being found willingly among
the black youths, they claimed they had been raped repeatedly by them. Locked away in the Scottsboro, Alabama,
prison awaiting trial, the "Scottsboro Boys" looked to be
prime lynching material—dirt poor, illiterate, and of highly
questionable moral character, even for teenagers; one of the
defendants had an advanced case of syphilis.

Told of the news, the NAACP engaged the only willing attorney in the area to assist in the hearing while it decided
whether to take on the case. At 69 Fifth Avenue the Scottsboro Boys—hardly aspiring professionals like the Sweet family or blameless victims like the Lowmans—didn't inspire
much pity among the likes of Mary White Ovington, White,
and even Du Bois. What evidence they could glean at first
made it seem like the boys had actually raped the girls in
question, and as Ovington later admitted, the organization
"did not want to defend boys guilty of rape." White had just
published a book arguing that rape was overstated as a cause
for lynching, and the NAACP had been built on the idea of connecting the best whites with the best blacks to lead the way
together. Defending these nine would risk destroying what
fragile coalition the NAACP had built with Southern liberals
and Northern power brokers. Besides, the two prerequisites
for the NAACP to take on a case were, according to White, an
injustice based on race and the possibility of setting a legal
precedent. Early on it wasn't clear that either one was met in
the case of the Scottsboro Boys. As Kenneth Janken points

out, "The NAACP was not a social service agency, White believed; rather it was in the business of helping blacks organize themselves to fight for equality."

Within two weeks, eight of the Scottsboro Boys (one had
turned state's evidence) had been found guilty of rape and sentenced to death. Their trials, quick and messy, were only a
notch above lynch mobs, but the defendants had done themselves no favors, at times admitting the crimes, then pleading their innocence and blaming the others. As White and his
board continued mulling things over, in walked the Communist Party of the United States, kicking off ten months of confusion and conflict that reflects poorly on almost everyone
involved, and shattering the lives of the Scottsboro Boys.

While history has assigned the blame for the NAACP's
many missteps in this case largely to White, the problems
began with the hesitation of the entire leadership. Devoted
as they were to the cause of civil rights, they were relatively
insulated from the devastation of the depression and the impact it would have on their organization. Outside, America
was flying apart. In Harlem and Philadelphia, black unemployment ran at 50 percent. Apocalypse was in the wind;
many felt that capitalism had run its course. Demagogues
such as Father Coughlin and Huey Long found ready follow-
ers. Even moderates called for a new order, and one of the
first things to go was the genteel reformism that had given
rise to the NAACP. The white-collar glad-handing that White
specialized in was creating a disconnect between the NAACP
and the broader population of black America now asking
for sweeping change. Communism and the Soviet paradise
were getting a hard look from Americans black and white.
Even Mississippi senator Theodore Bilbo, unreconstructed
to the core, admitted, "I'm getting a little pink myself." The
Scottsboro case offered the Communists their chance to
show what they could offer "the masses."

Everyone watched to see how the NAACP, an organization kept afloat by capitalists, would play it. But the hesitation continued. "I had waited eagerly for Walter to grab the case," wrote Wilkins, "but to my surprise, the New York office seemed inclined to let it go by." Deciding that the case was simply another Elaine, Arkansas, the board denied White's request to go down to investigate, and hoped to handle it quietly with local lawyers. Then the prosecution crushed the first line of defense provided by the NAACP, a pair of incompetent attorneys, one who appeared drunk at a hearing and the other too meek to claim he was actually involved. The Communists sent representatives of the International Legal Defense (ILD) to the jail and soon announced that they'd convinced the families they were best suited to handle the appeals.

White then rushed to Kirby Prison in Birmingham and met with the defendants and their families, meetings that went poorly. The differences were acute: the light-skinned, high-caste, urban, social-climbing White sitting in a prison cell with indigent, uneducated Southern blacks of a sort whose lives had changed only marginally since the end of slavery. His powers of persuasion, so effective on Capitol Hill, could only move the Scottsboro Boys at best to reconsider NAACP involvement. They were "illiterate," claimed a stung Walter White afterward, just ignorant country folk impressed by the white Communists. The distaste was mutual. Hearing White's comments, Mamie Williams, the mother of one of the defendants, responded that they were "not too ignorant to know that if we let the NAACP look after our boys, that they will die."

What neither organization wanted was a united defense, though the NAACP would later claim it had suggested that. Each wanted full control of the case, the agenda, and the money. For nine months they ran parallel fund-raising campaigns and filed various briefs and motions until the whole thing became, as White called it, "a badly tangled state of affairs." Until this point the Communist party and the NAACP had co-existed peaceably. In September 1930, for example, White had testified before Congress that the NAACP was neutral toward the American Communist party. Many of the brightest lights of the Harlem Renaissance had leaned left, and Du Bois understood the attraction of communism and had visited the Soviet Union in its early days, so there were many links between the two camps. They had marched together in generally the same direction until the depression, at which point the money that kept them both going began to dry up. The Garland Fund award may have prompted the Communists to begin to working actively against NAACP interests—losing the $100,000 had been a blow. But the Soviets themselves, seeing the enormous ideological opening of the Great Depression, had directed the American party to act more aggressively on African-American issues. A vocal and attractive vanguard of black intellectuals, led by Langston Hughes and Paul Robeson, pulled black thought hard to the left in the thirties, and the Communist party poured energy into grassroots activism. On the ground in Harlem and elsewhere, the party now promoted itself as the defender of the average African American. It did indeed provide tangible support along with its rhetoric for serious, revolutionary change of a kind the NAACP had only nibbled at. Whether or not Stalin and the Communists truly cared about the fate of the Scottsboro defendants beyond their publicity value (the same question sometimes leveled at the NAACP) is debatable.

The battle continued into the summer, with the various defendants changing their minds and shifting their defense from one group to the other. Revelations made it obvious that the two accusers were no models of Southern purity and had most likely lied. Alarm bells grew louder, and public opinion worse, when the NAACP refused to accept a case in July involving black sharecroppers who had been attacked while trying to organize. The NAACP blamed the episode on Communist agitators. In August the white-shoe firm engaged by the NAACP in the Scottsboro case finally threw up its hands. White, in all but despair, turned to Clarence Darrow. "The situation is so tense," White wrote Lampkin, "that it would not at all surprise me if a very bloody race riot broke loose." To him, it was still just a legal case, not a cause, but Wilkins argued that White needed to think less about guilt or innocence and more about a big-picture publicity strategy, a campaign like Parker and anti-lynching. Wilkins claims the secretary handed the whole deal off to him in August. "When I reached New York and took my new job he told me, 'Roy, the Scottsboro Case is your baby.'" But as much as White may have wanted to wash his hands of it, he was too much the amateur lawyer, and he couldn't run away.

Although he would become a committed Communist later in his life, Du Bois at this point was if not more anti-Communist than White, then more eloquently so. He wrote a damning piece about the party's role in the Scottsboro case in *The Crisis*, much of which would appear under White's name later that year in *Harper's* magazine. But White's management of the case was driving Du Bois mad. In over his head, outplayed by Reds and country folk, White was missing a chance to put to rest a political and economic theory that Du Bois felt at that point had no meaning for the real lives of African Americans.

White was not a counterpuncher. Throughout his career he had relied on the element of surprise, on throwing everything up for grabs, and he continued to see the NAACP in those terms when in fact, to most blacks, he and the NAACP were now the "suits." All he could do in response to the Communists' peppery approach was to make phone calls and wring his hands about legal precedent when what was most needed was a protective arm.

That he had to fight fellow leftists rather than right-wing racists was also galling. All through the twenties and thirties White had enjoyed extensive contacts and friendships with Communists that did not end with the Scottsboro case, and young Marxists such as Ralph Bunche would still look to the NAACP later in the decade as the best vehicle for their ideas. But the times were transforming intellectual leftism into class warfare. As much as White was an interlocutor between races, he was also one between classes, spending his days among wealthy people, surely coveting their lifestyles but also knowing them as individuals. He had been raised in a time and a place when black men rose up through business while the labor movement spent most of its efforts trying to steal their jobs. Since then the Communist party had done nothing to show it had anything more than its own political agenda in mind, so why should African Americans trust choices made for them thousands of miles away in snowy Moscow, any more than those the Populists had made? The American system, White believed, could work fine for blacks if they were ever given full access to it. Stuck between rich and poor as surely as he was between black and white, White voted Socialist in 1932.

That fall was a nightmare. In October the Garland Fund notified the NAACP that the economic downturn had damaged its investments to such a degree that it would not be able to honor the $100,000 award, putting the Margold Plan in jeopardy and throwing the NAACP back on the mercy of its branches just as popular support was dwindling. Rumblings in the NAACP office, led by Du Bois, Pickens, and Seligman, grew louder. Then, in November, personal tragedy struck. Just days after White claimed that the Scottsboro situation "looks better than ever," George White was hit by a car as he crossed the corner of Houston and Piedmont in Atlanta. Rushed to a white hospital in that segregated city, he was stabilized until Madeline and their son-in-law discovered him. Both darker than George, their appearance made the hospital staff realize they'd taken in a black person and promptly had George removed to a black facility. A week later, on November 19, Walter sat vigil as his father ebbed away and finally died in early December. As a final insult, while White slept on the train back to New York, he was robbed.

Without a penny in his pocket or a shred of identification, White did not head to 409 Edgecombe and his family. Instead he fell straight into the arms of Poppy Cannon, a woman who, unlike Gladys, always had a smile, if not a deep thought. In her book *A Gentle Knight* she describes him weeping for his father, furious at the injustice, that the doctors at the white hospital had called George "a nigger" and all but sentenced him to death. Cannon's recollection is sketchy—she has White as Johnson's assistant when he's already secretary, for example—and her telling of George's story relies on White's own telling in *A Man Called White*, doubtful itself in certain details. What is entirely credible, though, is White cracking under the pressure. Cannon doesn't admit that the affair began here, but the two of them soon cooked up a book project for Knopf about black cuisine that allowed them plausible time together. Cannon and Joel Spingarn's wife Hope then went off on a research trip to the South, including a stop in Atlanta, where Madeline met Poppy—according to Walter's sister Helen, against her mother's will, though Cannon wrote that they "got along famously." Considering that Walter had never taken Gladys to Atlanta, the visit must have raised a flag. White dropped the project soon after, and they broke off.

Poppy had much to console Walter about during that first flush of romance. Later that month Clarence Darrow pulled out of the Scottsboro case. The ILD wanted him to work under their direction, with no ties to the NAACP, and Darrow refused. Cutting its losses, the NAACP disengaged entirely from the Scottsboro case in January 1932. To the puzzlement of Johnson, watching from afar, White claimed victory, saying that everyone would know their eventual freedom would come from a Supreme Court decision based on *Moore v. Dempsey*. "Not one person in a thousand," Johnson replied, "would either hear or understand the basis on which the victory might be won." The only consolation White could take was that, grateful as they were for the Communists' efforts in Alabama, and open to, even begging for, new economic strategies, African Americans had not jumped aboard the Communist bandwagon en masse. In 1930 there had been six thousand members of the American Communist party, and now there were twelve thousand, with blacks only a fraction of them. Like White, they were largely pragmatists, which meant he still had a chance to win them back.

*

But first he would have to win back his own organization. With the economy spiraling down in late 1931 and the Garland Fund money suddenly gone, the board, based on White's numbers, recommended significant pay cuts. The NAACP would now also assume editorial control of *The Crisis*. Other executives were not doing enough to raise money, claimed White, while he was. The response from Du Bois was strong, and personal. In late December, as the Scottsboro case crumbled in White's hands, Du Bois delivered a letter to the board signed by Bagnall, Pickens, Wilkins, and Seligman. White and Ovington, they said, had cooked the books. The real problem was White's high-end travel, his wasteful attitude toward money as it concerned *him*, and his dreadful management style. "We have all had considerable and varied experiences," they stated, "but in our several careers, we have never met a man like Walter White who under an outward and charming manner has succeeded within a short time in alienating and antagonizing every one of his co-workers, including all the clerks in the office."

White wobbled, but if the insurgents had hoped the board would fire him immediately, they were wrong. For all the places where the board concurred with their views—"Mr. White does not care to ask another's opinion, certainly not mine," wrote Ovington. "I do not always feel that he is just to others"—Du Bois carried at least as much baggage as White. *The Crisis*, once the engine room of the NAACP, now bled money when money was needed most, and Du Bois was burning through his fund of goodwill. He rarely attended board meetings. Now this letter, its petulance, and his shot at Ovington annoyed the board more than White's ineptitude. At least White was functional; Du Bois started more fires than he put out. This one was all but inevitable since Du Bois had butted heads with everyone in power at the NAACP at some point. By now White was "worth ten times as much to us," wrote Ovington to Arthur Spingarn (her use of "us" an insight into how she viewed the NAACP), a painful assessment given how close she had once been to Du Bois.

Still, there was truth to Du Bois's charges, and even as the rebellious staffers stood back from their letter, an outside auditor was brought in to assess the workings of the group and broker a peace. Although the board supported White and he kept his position, the report three months later amounted to a negative performance review. Considering the budget pressures, White's travel expenses were extreme and vaguely accounted for, especially as salaries were being cut. He needed to see the branches as more than just a source of revenue, and the NAACP as a whole had to react to the depression with a greater attention to economics. In the office White would have to treat the staff differently, and he would no longer have oversight of *The Crisis*; in fact, Du Bois would join the COA. He'd won the round; White had been put on notice.

*

Two years of internal struggle followed for the direction and management of the NAACP. Du Bois, along with young economists and thinkers such as Ralph Bunche, John Davis, and Abram Harris, tried to push the organization toward economic issues that until then had been the province of the Urban League. White now had to fight for more than his ideas; he had to fight for his job. The year 1932 passed with the secretary under a sort of regency, blamed for a lack of vision when the vision he believed in, the Margold Plan, had been stymied by the depression. The NAACP lurched through the year, like everyone else in America desperately searching for certainty and direction. Du Bois's tenure was as shaky as White's: even closing down *The Crisis* was discussed. Support drained at a frightening rate. An NAACP survey of the black press revealed impatience with the organization's constant need for top billing at a time when all hands had to work together.

Few alternatives were forthcoming, though, and certainly not from White. Knowing that he'd probably be out if Du Bois won, but also with a sincere conviction that civil rights, not just economics, were at the crux of black advancement, White dug in. "In my first years as Walter White's assistant, I tried hard and without much success to talk the NAACP into expanding its programs," Roy Wilkins recalled. Joel Spingarn suggested a second Amenia Conference, and even his friend Dr. Louis T. Wright warned him that things had to change. Although White did advance a number of economic initiatives, such as joining a consortium of groups to protest Hoover's hiring practices at the Boulder Dam, he pursued economic issues on a case-by-case basis, without the underlying strategy and philosophy of the Margold Plan, his chosen direction. While he agreed in principle with much of what the young economists said, the NAACP couldn't afford to push both politics and economics. In this approach White may have looked to Atlanta. In 1926 Eugene Martin, an executive at Atlanta Life, had married White's sister Helen and begun a lifelong friendship that would see Martin eventually join the national board of the NAACP. When the depression hit, Atlanta Life had concentrated on reducing risk in all ways to weather the storm, and White now took the same tack, avoiding anything radical, conserving resources, and pushing the tried and true. White's polarizing personality, though, gave his opponents the upper hand in the contest for control and money.

The emergence of Franklin D. Roosevelt as the Democratic nominee for the White House only complicated matters. Although Hoover had spent his entire career ignoring the needs of African Americans, Roosevelt considered Georgia his second home and was counting on Southern support to win, putting men like "Cotton" Ed Smith and Theodore Bilbo in the driver's seat. That summer White even reached out to Hoover with advice on winning the black vote, and though the president ignored it, the NAACP nonetheless endorsed him in 1932. FDR's landslide election sent shivers through the black community, who agreed with White and had voted overwhelmingly for Hoover.

The darkest days were now upon White and black America. With unemployment across the nation at 25 percent, incomes halved, and wages dropping through the floor, Hoover orchestrated an uneasy transition of power that helped provoke a run on the banking system. Through his Hundred Days legislative attack starting in March, FDR stabilized the

nation and begin the recovery process with the National Recovery Act (NRA), agricultural reform, the Civilian Conser-
vation Corps (CCC), and other programs that provided relief
and reinvigoration. Unfortunately, black America's worst
fears about a president with Southern sympathies came
true. Relief was apportioned so that whites received the major share, even though black Americans had been hit harder.
Segregation was enforced throughout all jobs programs, and
when restructuring and limits on businesses demanded lay-
offs and firings, blacks were usually the first to go. Disease
and hunger ravaged the rural South, followed by the Dust
Bowl in the summer of 1933. Something had to happen. This
would be the fulcrum year for White and the NAACP.

*

For Walter White, at least, the darkest had come before the
dawn. Although FDR's early policies drove African Americans further down and the president's advisers steered him
away from any small bit of help he may have been inclined
to offer them, events began to conspire in White's favor, and
in ways that would ultimately benefit black America. In January he responded to Scottsboro and the populist impulse by
trying to interest Arthur Spingarn in expanding the NAACP's
legal defense program to include criminals. This initiative
went nowhere, but two cases argued by Charles Houston,
the first black editor of the *Harvard Law Review*, and William Hastie helped White's legal strategy take root.

In the first case Houston was able temporarily to block
the extradition of George Crawford to Virginia to face murder
charges on the grounds that he could not be tried by a jury
of his peers because blacks were not allowed on grand juries
in that state. When the decision was overturned, White used
Houston to defend Crawford, establishing the precedent of
black lawyers trying NAACP cases. The case was a near disas-

ter; all the evidence had led White and the lawyers to believe in Crawford's innocence, but when surprise evidence came out implicating him, the best Houston could do was save him from the electric chair.

The second case was also a pyrrhic victory, but a victory all the same. When Thomas Hocutt, a young waiter, was denied admission to the University of North Carolina School of Pharmacy, the NAACP sued for his entry. Although the case was lost on a technicality, the judge made it clear that he might have ruled otherwise, inspiring White to push further on education cases, over the objections of Ovington and many others on the board. Among the lawyers assisting on the Crawford case was Thurgood Marshall, who together with Houston and Hastie would soon form the core of the NAACP legal defense team. In May the American Fund promised $20,000 to support interstate travel and education cases: the NAACP had taken the first steps toward *Brown v. Board of Education*. Although the seeds of the strategy could be found in James Weldon Johnson's handling of the Sweet case in 1925, White now staked his career on the conviction that education cases and the Margold Plan should remain the NAACP's top priority.

Meanwhile Du Bois and the economics proponents strengthened their hand. In March, Joel Spingarn announced his resignation from the board, dismayed by the direction White was taking the NAACP. To placate the board president, with whom White had a pronounced love/hate relationship, in August he grudgingly assembled the second Amenia Conference at Spingarn's estate in Dutchess County, New York, not far from FDR's Hyde Park. Despite the encouraging legal developments that would in time lead to so much, the black leaders at the retreat decided that the old philosophies and approaches no longer worked. While explicitly rejecting communism, the conference authorized Abram Harris, the young economist who had recently published the influential book *The Black Worker*, to lead the Committee on Future Plan and Program and reinvent the NAACP along economic lines. Du Bois, who by now had moved from New York to Fisk University in Atlanta, helpfully suggested that all paid executives such as White be laid off. (That this would place all the NAACP's power and day-to-day functions back in the hands of wealthy white philanthropists and pro bono white lawyers apparently mattered less to Du Bois than getting rid of his nemesis.)

The NAACP had taken a radical step, but the moment for radical action was about to pass. While the first New Deal of 1933 hurt black America, it established the difficult but pragmatic goal of preserving both capitalism and democracy at a time when Russia, Germany, and Italy had run to their separate extremes of fascism and communism. At the annual convention that spring, the NAACP membership had voiced their desire for more action but had stopped short of asking for the kind of radical change that Du Bois and Harris were pursuing. After all, as the entire economic system shuddered through talk of coups and dictators and revolution, the Constitution still stood. And it was the Constitution that White, whether consciously or not, relied on, pitting the possibility of its full and equal application against an unrealistic scenario of black America driving the national economic discussion in the face of institutional racism.

*

The depression had one more deadly effect on black Americans: economic pressure ignited white-on-black violence. Many—White included—believed that lynching had all but ended, but ten victims in 1929 had risen to twenty-eight in 1933, with a particularly horrific spate that fall. Although he now accepted the reality that the Committee on Future Plan was moving ahead (or said he did, even acknowledging to Du Bois in a letter that this was a "transitional period"), the strange fruit in the autumn trees made clear that all the old problems hadn't disappeared. This renewed violence nonetheless created an opportunity. Under pressure from the outside and within, White decided it was time for another attempt at an anti-lynching bill. His contention with the Harris Plan had less to do with content than control; Harris wanted the fundamental mission of the NAACP to change, and an anti-lynching campaign would allow White to operate from strength. After all, he'd made his name fighting lynching. A galvanizing black issue that had nothing to do with economic competition against whites or political theories, anti-lynching would, strategically speaking, put the game back onto his field. Virtually everyone was against lynching, which made it a proven fund-raiser, and it would flush out FDR. Other groups without the NAACP's track record were floating the same idea, and even James Weldon Johnson confirmed White's instinct that this was the time.

The board, many of whom were as leery as White of the proposed restructuring, agreed with the secretary. A December meeting, chaired by the NAACP, brought together a range of organizations that now committed to a single anti-lynching bill, to be driven by NAACP leadership. Energized and at the wheel, White brought to bear all his old strategies. He reached out to Southern moderates such as Will Alexander of the Commission on Interracial Cooperation, now also working within the administration, and Jesse Daniel Ames of the Association of Southern Women for the Prevention of Lynching. For all their talk, these white groups had an almost geological sense of gradualism and would ultimately hinder more than help; but their involvement solidified white support. In New York White enlisted his old friend Nella Larsen to lead the Independent Writers' League Against Lynching, which included names such as Sherwood Anderson, Edna Ferber, and Dorothy Parker. (After two years of writers like Dos Passos and Dreiser banging the drum for the Communist party, this must have been a great joy for White.) A draft bill was ready by the end of the year, to be introduced in the Senate by Democrats Robert Wagner of New York and Colorado's Edward Costigan, both liberals and well embedded in the New Deal. The bill differed from the Dyer Bill in that it did not make lynching a federal crime as long as local authorities fully prosecuted it.

As White lined up witnesses for the hearings, he made his most influential friend. In January 1934 Eleanor Roosevelt, charged by her husband with working the softer issues of the New Deal but driven by a sharpening of her own sense of social justice, hosted a dinner for a group of distinguished black leaders that included John Hope and Charles Johnson as well as White. During an unprecedented four-hour, candid discussion of how the New Deal was punishing black Americans, White hit it off with the first lady on a personal level and sold her on himself and the cause. In the years ahead she would offer him a channel to the Oval Office. More important, the meeting opened the White House as never before to black voices and black interests. Not yet institutional, it was the sort of back-channel stuff that White loved. Mrs. Roosevelt signaled a full commitment to raising her husband's awareness of African-American issues. Her immediate willingness to help White with the anti-lynching bill boosted his stature as well as the bill's chances in the Senate.

Sensing the shift, Du Bois fought back. That month's issue of *The Crisis* featured a piece entitled "Segregation," in which Du Bois argued a position not far from that of his old enemy, Booker T. Washington. While not blatantly advocating segregation, Du Bois declared that African Americans should strike out on a path of self-reliance and even self-segregation rather than wait for white acceptance. As they had at other times since the end of the Civil War, blacks needed to focus on their own survival, not fantasies of assimilation that were really available only to black elites. This was heresy to White, who furiously responded that Du Bois was offering ammunition to white separatists and confusing the powers that be just as he'd launched a campaign of personal diplomacy with the first lady. To him, guaranteeing personal liberty for all was the great tradition, the purpose, of the NAACP. The battle for resources and control had now become philosophical: Was self-segregation the same as segregation? Or was it segregation only if it was forced? Should the goal of African Americans be to join as full participants in the larger culture and economy, or should it be to preserve a separate culture within it? Should change come from the bottom up or the top down, or in the end did that really matter? These are important questions still debated today, and the work of both White and Du Bois as politicians, thinkers, and artists now allows most African Americans to decide them for themselves. But how the NAACP answered these questions in the mid-thirties largely determined the direction of civil rights for the following two decades. Over the next six months the conflict would come to a head and leave one man at the top of the NAACP.

Tussling with Du Bois on his flank, White attended the two days of Senate hearings for the Costigan-Wagner Bill in February, testifying at length on the history of lynching in the United States, the Dyer Bill, and the growing sentiment throughout all sections of the country for anti-lynching legislation. Other witnesses covered a wide range of interests, from academia and the bar to Southern religious leaders and the arts. The masterstroke, though, was the result of another example of White's prescient understanding of media.

An anonymous donor paid to have the proceedings broadcast live by the NBC Radio Network, the first time Senate hearings were heard live. The Senate committee quickly returned with a favorable report; prospects were promising.

With White on the rise, Du Bois now went for the kill. Printing the secretary's rebuttal in the March issue of *The Crisis*, he countered with a series of reasoned arguments, then revealed his true feelings: "In the first place, Walter White is white." Free as White was to do as he pleased, according to Du Bois he had no relation to or knowledge of the problems of black Americans. By no means was Du Bois the first to have this thought—it had certainly been aired in Harlem during the twenties, especially as White cozied up to Van Vechten and other artsy white swells—but to voice it publicly at a crucial moment, to employ it within the context of a serious and valid interchange, was an act of self-immolation by Du Bois, and profoundly damaging to the internal reform he championed for the NAACP. In an organization where associates of twenty years addressed each other in memoranda as "Miss Ovington" and "Mr. Spingarn," Du Bois had crossed every line. Led by James Weldon Johnson, whose wife Grace Nail was nearly as fair skinned as White, the board rallied behind White and censored Du Bois, igniting yet another firefight. Against all this, White added the gun incident to his unpublished narrative of racial enlightenment.

Meanwhile the Costigan-Wagner Bill, after a promising start, languished under expected resistance from the Southern senators FDR still needed to continue his programs. The president did nothing to move the bill forward. Eleanor Roosevelt now began to meet regularly with White, and their friendship blossomed. By spring White had fifty-two votes in his pocket and needed only vocal support from the president to push the bill through. After some resistance from FDR's

White (left) visiting James Weldon Johnson and Johnson's wife, Grace Nail, in Great Barrington, Massachusetts. Both Johnson and Grace White Ovington kept country homes in the same Berkshires town where Du Bois was born. *(Yale Collection of American Literature, Beinecke Rare Book and Manuscript Library)*

staff, the first lady finally arranged a private conference between White and the president on May 6. After a brief prep with Eleanor, White sipped tea on the White House porch with Roosevelt, his wife, and his mother. For an hour and twenty minutes he parried, first, FDR's usual strategy of telling amusing stories to avoid unpleasant topics, and then, second, the president's fear of losing the Southern support he needed to continue the New Deal. He was trying to save the country, he said, and pushing the Southern senators too hard would kill his efforts. Although he promised to urge a vote before adjournment, he wouldn't try to break a filibuster. Eleanor Roosevelt wrote later that White could not hide his disappointment. "You go ahead," she reports FDR saying to White, "you do everything you can do. Whatever you can get done is okay with me, but I just can't do it."

Afterward, White expressed great optimism despite the meeting's bad turn, probably hoping to save face. But the days passed suspiciously with no word from the White House. Costigan and Wagner followed up with the president while White, increasingly frustrated, considered more public protests, once planting a reporter to ambush the president at a press conference with a question about the bill. The session of Congress ended without action. Furious, Charles Houston reminded White that he'd warned him FDR would "chisel in a pinch." Still, there was achievement. White had not forced the bill into law, but he'd gotten closer than Johnson ever had on Capitol Hill. He had found a place for himself within the White House family, another blurry, border area between power and his constituency. And he had learned to trust Eleanor Roosevelt, who was finding her own values within the administration and voicing them more often, proving herself willing to match the loyalty White had shown her with her own. The president, on the other hand, was not to be trusted.

That July, just weeks after Congress adjourned, Du Bois resigned from the NAACP. White's meeting with the president may have been a crowning moment for the secretary, but it epitomized all that Du Bois had come to dislike about White and question about the organization. Du Bois no longer believed in the NAACP's strategy, if ever he fully had. "The battle of my people must be a moral one, not a legal or physical one," he wrote. White, on the other hand, clearly shared Niebuhr's belief that "All social co-operation on a larger scale than the most intimate social group requires a measure of coercion." While completely understandable in terms of personalities, the split was tragic in that both men believed the struggle for civil rights was a moral one. Like any war, though, there were many fronts. Each fought on his chosen front with skill, determination, and often genius, but they rarely appreciated that in each other, nor would they ever join forces in the coordinated way that would have let the NAACP fight on all fronts at once. Although resources were at the center of this dispute, the depth of their mutual distaste, wrapped in philosophy but intensely personal, was the ultimate cause. Ovington was relieved, but Joel Spingarn finally went through with his resignation and White stacked the board with loyalists such as Dr. Louis T. Wright and famed music impresario John Hammond.

That summer, as Abram Harris hammered out the details of the Committee on the Future Plan and Program, White had already consolidated his power. The program would be passed in 1935, but the board would leave it to the secretary to implement, effectively ending the reform movement. In the years ahead the NAACP would pursue economic justice on White's terms, as part of the New Deal coalition. Correct as Harris, John Davis, and other leftists within the NAACP may have been on economic theory, practical—and sometimes personal—politics were driving the recovery. While the Roosevelt administration had damaged the interests of black America during the first round of the New Deal, behind the scenes Eleanor was now prodding her husband toward a more inclusive government as economic prospects rose.

Familiar faces, sympathetic to the cause, began to appear in the administration. So far the one favor Roosevelt had done black America was to name Harold Ickes, former head of the Chicago NAACP, as secretary of the interior. Ickes had desegregated the department in 1933, encouraging other departments to follow suit, and had hired Edwin Embree, head of the Rosenwald Fund that had long and generously subsidized the NAACP. Frank Murphy, the former judge in the Sweet case who'd maintained a friendship with White, was close to Roosevelt and would soon be his attorney general. The distinguished educator Mary McLeod Bethune came aboard in October 1934 as a special representative for black affairs and by 1936 had formed an informal "Black Cabinet." The first lady announced the official desegregation of the White House quarters and now could be seen ambling through the Rose Garden arm-in-arm with Bethune, scandalizing the old Southern hands.

A page was being turned. Only one, and at the beginning of a long story, but it was being turned. The moderate approach that Harris wanted to move past was precisely the one used by the New Dealers, mostly middle-class pragmatists and capitalists. At his core, White was a New Dealer too. He believed in the American system, and as the interests of the black elite most mirrored the concerns of the white middle class, he looked for stability and reform, not revolution. That involved operating again in that borderland between principle and practicality where he had been raised and worked best. He aligned the NAACP with the Second New Deal, fighting against discrimination and for more opportunities in government agencies that controlled thousands of jobs, and maintaining an independent position from which his organization could publicly criticize and challenge FDR every time he claimed his hands were tied. Then as now, the federal government functioned with thousands of small decisions and responsibilities. Those kinds of decisions— matters of fiat open to the influence of a charming phone call and some moral suasion—were in White's comfort zone. With his connections to the first lady, to Congress from lobbying for Costigan-Wagner, and to Bethune's Black Cabinet, White helped permeate the administration with a sense of responsibility to its black citizens not seen since Reconstruction.

The downside of doing business this way was the compromises it required. White often pulled his punches and accepted less than he wanted from the administration, leaving him open to charges of selling out to the New Deal. But his goal was getting as much as he could now, cutting his losses, and moving on to the next play. Gradual as this method was, it was realistic, and the end point, *Brown v. Board of Education*, must be seen at least in some degree as a vindication of his strategy. Nor was it all theory: between 1930 and 1939, life expectancy for black men rose from forty-seven years to fifty-two and for black women from forty-nine to fifty-five. Infant mortality dropped from 100 per thousand to 73. Achieving access to employment, relief, and health care, it can be argued, had a huge impact on these figures. By the time of the 1934 midterm election, despite an editorial in *The Crisis* by Oswald Garrison Villard blasting the New Deal, blacks voted overwhelmingly for FDR, beginning their long association with the Democratic party and solidifying the president's coalition.

Ever sensitive to shifts in power, Carl Van Vechten made sure to invite White to dinner with Gertrude Stein and Alice B. Toklas when they visited New York in the fall to see the production of her play *Four Saints in 3 Acts*. Never one to hold a grudge, White happily attended, and to his last days claimed a special fondness for Alice's chocolate mousse recipe. People such as Nella Larsen, Eugene Saxton, and even Du Bois never disappeared from White's life, especially if they could be useful to him. To the ideologues, White's ability to move on without rancor may appear duplicitous, but to an organization man like White it simply made sense. Being an organization man doesn't indicate lockstep behavior; it requires improvisation, adjustment, reversal, alliances, and betrayals. It spoke to an instinct White had, or at least a knowledge that men can change, that they're not always who their resumés say they are. Many African Americans were incensed by his endorsement of former Klan member

Hugo Black for the Supreme Court in 1937. Perhaps because eleven years before, he'd seen a man in Aiken, South Carolina, take off his hood and repent for what he'd done, White believed there was more to Black. Once on the bench, Black proved White correct as a consistent supporter of civil rights. Personal knowledge meant more to White than principle.

*

For the next four years White continued to push for anti-lynching legislation, with diminishing results in Congress but an ever-increasing national profile for himself and the NAACP. Now in control of the organization, he faced a new kind of pressure in the fall of 1934. Black Americans deserved something from the White House for their electoral support, and it was now up to White, the moral courtier to the first lady, to deliver it for them. The lynching of Claude Neal late in October, a grotesque, all-night session of torture and summary execution in Florida, seemed the perfect opportunity for FDR to vindicate White's faith in his people's political and moral weight. But where he'd hoped to hear finally a ringing endorsement of Costigan-Wagner, White heard nothing from the White House, and the Justice Department chose not to pursue an investigation. When White begged the first lady to attend a rally, she declined, with regrets, under orders from the president. A December warning from Leonidas Dyer, Republican sponsor of the original bill back in the twenties, that the Democrats were playing black Americans for fools, was ringing sadly true.

Again and again, White pleaded his case with Mrs. Roosevelt, passing along letters and clippings from the black press threatening a quick end to support for her husband. Costigan introduced the bill again in January, to silence from the president. Although FDR claimed through his wife to be quietly buttonholing senators, he refused to take a public stand. As ever, White worked every angle, whipping up all the publicity he could, including an anti-lynching art show at a New York gallery featuring works by Reginald Marsh, Thomas Hart Benton, George Bellows, and others. Invited as the guest of honor to the opening, again the first lady had to decline and instead sneaked in for a private viewing. On Capitol Hill Southern senators filibustered the bill until Costigan finally yielded in April so that FDR could put through the slate of the Second New Deal, which included the Social Security Act and the Works Progress Administration.

Embarrassed, White resigned the seat the president had given him on the Virgin Islands Advisory Council. "In justice to the cause I serve," White wrote to Roosevelt, "I cannot continue to remain even a small part of your official family." And yet, more than ever, he was. The genuine and mutual friendship he shared with the first lady, the passion he had inspired in her for this bill and for the cause of civil rights in general, was putting pressure on her relationship with her husband and within the White House. Roosevelt's racist gatekeepers, press secretary Steve Early and Marvin McIntyre, detested White. As the NAACP head harangued the president's office with letters and telegrams that August, in hopes of seeing the bill reintroduced, Early demanded that the first lady's staff call him off, describing him as "one of the worst and most continuous of troublemakers" and finding many of his letters "decidedly insulting." Eleanor remained loyal and uncowed: her friend, she told Early, a descendant of the legendary Confederate general Jubal Early, had "the sorrows of his people close to his heart." While FDR relied on his wife to be his conscience, her pursuit of justice for black Americans proceeded too fast and too far for his comfort.

*

As time passed with no anti-lynching bill to show for its efforts, the expected criticism arose that the NAACP had thrown in too heavily with FDR and seen nothing in return. The Second New Deal was more inclusive only relative to what had existed before, and certainly not by modern standards. With his major energies focused on anti-lynching, White addressed economics and the legal campaign with modular solutions. Charles Houston was hired full time in 1935 to run the legal department. After a major victory in 1938 in the *Gaines* decision, outlawing discrimination in public universities, the NAACP spun off the Legal Defense and Educational Fund. Covering the purview of the Margold Plan and the widening interests of black Americans, the fund raised money on its own and developed an autonomy in the coming decades as it drove toward *Brown v. Board of Education*. Although his devotion to legal remedy has contributed to White's historical neglect, it made the Legal Defense Fund possible.

The economic solution was not as clean. In 1933 two young economists named John Davis and Robert Weaver had created an organization to monitor New Deal programs for their application to African Americans, and to petition the administration. With the NAACP, other groups pooled funds that allowed Davis and Weaver to build the Joint Committee on National Recovery (JCNR) and lobby the White House and Congress on economic issues. Weaver was soon tapped by the Department of the Interior to work on black affairs, and though Davis's freewheeling nature and leftist inclinations concerned White, his in-depth research and generally practical application of his findings proved valuable. In 1934 an NAACP committee was formed to explore folding the JCNR completely into the organization. Davis could not be controlled, though, and it's possible White was simply offering his own alternative to the Harris program being hashed out at the time. By 1935 the idea was scrapped, and Davis went on to play a role in the birth of a competing organization, the National Negro Congress (NNC), driven by the Communist party.

White's economic policy, such as it was, continued to rely on the underlying principles of the New Deal, with the secretary satisfied to criticize loudly, waving the cudgel of black votes as a threat. Organized labor offered little hope. After the Parker hearings in 1930, White had suggested reaching out to the American Federation of Labor (AFL), which had played a role in defeating Hoover's nominee. But the effort went nowhere, and the stalemate between blacks and labor continued. Union membership swelled with the Labor Relations Act of 1934 that gave all workers the right to organize, and when the Congress of Industrial Organizations (CIO) stepped away from the leftist politics of old labor and announced that it would work within the constructs of capitalism and be color-blind, a breakthrough looked possible. The reality in Washington and in the factories, though, was different. Again FDR and the New Dealers backed down in the face of racist elements and never forced anti-discrimination language into the Labor Relations Act. Meanwhile the big unions remained willing to limit their strength as long as it satisfied their racism. The NAACP would encourage union membership among African Americans, but mutual hostility prevented any real thaw.

*

With the searing disappointment of 1935 still in mind, White pressed for another meeting with FDR and got it in January 1936. Once again the president expressed his sympathy for

At the height of the campaign for anti-lynching legislation in 1937, White confers with William Hastie and Harlem's representative Joseph Gavagan. *(Library of Congress)*

White's goal but no help, and instead suggested a Senate investigation into lynching. To this end a proposal by Indiana senator Frederick Van Nuys was introduced in the Senate, and White, ever hopeful, pictured another public forum for the NAACP's views. And once again Southern senators blocked the action by cutting its funding. Between 1936 and 1940 White would choreograph three more attempts at anti-lynching legislation. The Gavagan Bill passed the House in 1937 but was filibustered in the Senate and ultimately pulled in favor of FDR's farm bill.

And in 1938 another full-blown Senate sideshow that lasted almost seven weeks put White on the cover of *Time* magazine, calling him "spunky," "dapper," and "the most potent leader of his race in the U.S." During his ramblings on the Senate floor, South Carolina's Jimmy Byrnes pointed up at the gallery where White could be found throughout the proceedings, and declared: "One Negro . . . has ordered this bill to pass and if a majority can pass it, it will pass. . . . If Walter White should consent to have this bill laid aside, its advocates would desert it as quickly as football players unscramble when the whistle of the referee is heard." Just as he'd been back in 1918, White was Public Enemy No. 1 for the Southern cracker. Flattering as that may have been, he was caught between a president who claimed never to have enough political capital to pass the bill, and nipping from the left in the form of Davis and the NNC, the rump of Communist influence in black America. Once committed, White had little choice but to persevere in order to preserve his position in the center of the storm.

The failure of the final bill, stymied again by Southern senators in winter of 1940, ended the NAACP's push for anti-lynching legislation. But White didn't just blame the Senate. In 1938 he had given producer David O. Selznick his comments on the script of *Gone with the Wind*, asking only for "accuracy" in how the film portrayed history; he was stunned by the final version and its whitewashing of slavery. White, who understood the powerful influence media had on public opinion, connected the dots. "Whatever sentiment there was in the South for Federal anti-lynch law," he said, "evaporated during the *Gone with the Wind* vogue."

To some observers, the years spent pressing for anti-lynching legislation had been wasted years, but in fact their net result was enormous. Public support for the legislation extended throughout the country, including the South, among all races and genders. A 1938 Gallup poll found that 72 percent of Americans, and 57 percent of Southerners, favored it. Under the banner of anti-lynching, White had created a wide coalition of like-minded groups that would form the foundation for the modern civil rights movement. Watching year after year the foul displays of filibustering senators,

Americans were disgusted by Southern racism after 1938. Although White could not, or would not choose to, catalyze mass action, the pieces were in place for a more dramatic shift in attitudes toward race in America. White considered a voting rights bill as the next battle, and a Republican administration under Wendell Wilkie may very well have used the bully pulpit of the presidency two decades before the entreaties of Lyndon Johnson. Whatever might have happened, though, was cleared aside by World War II. When evaluating the progress of movements and leaders, the things that cannot be controlled must be considered along with those that can.

*

As the decade drew to a close, White had vanquished many enemies, real and imagined. Du Bois was gone, having taken some of the black intelligentsia with him. The NAACP had awarded White the Spingarn Medal in 1937 for his life's work; in *A Man Called White* he describes with pride how Pidge, in his first long pants, stiffly stepped across the stage to "gravely" shake his father's hand. It's a grim picture, and more so because White doesn't realize it. Later that year, with the Communists long out of the picture, the NAACP arranged the release of four of the remaining Scottsboro Boys; White's brother-in-law Eugene Martin helped spirit them safely through Atlanta. James Weldon Johnson was killed in 1938, his car struck by a train in Florida. When Joel Spingarn died the next year, only Mary White Ovington and Arthur Spingarn remained of the old guard.

In January 1939 the Daughters of the American Revolution refused the black contralto Marian Anderson permission to give a concert in their Constitution Hall in Washington, D.C. For the next four months White built a wave of support for the singer within the world of the arts and

The White family in the late 1930s. *(Yale Collection of American Literature, Beinecke Rare Book and Manuscript Library)*

the black community. As the date of the original concert approached with still no venue, he had an idea: the steps of the Lincoln Memorial. Interior Secretary Ickes agreed, and on April 9, 1939, Anderson sang a concert—broadcast live on radio—before some 75,000 people. It created one of the most enduring images of black America in the 1930s and established the use of the Lincoln Memorial as a site for black inspiration and protest. When Martin Luther King delivered his "I Have a Dream" speech twenty-four years later, he was continuing a tradition and a trope envisioned and constructed by Walter White.

CHAPTER SIX

Fighting on All Fronts

꿔 As World War II rolled out across Europe and through the Far East, Walter White stood unchallenged at the top of the NAACP, in command of the most powerful black advocacy organization in America. Although he had used the anti-lynching campaign in the thirties to solidify that perception of the NAACP and enhance its influence, the issues surrounding civil rights and black Americans had multiplied in proportion to the complications of modern life. By 1940 a law against lynching wasn't strong enough to satisfy the aspirations of African Americans or materially improve their lives. Now White, flexible as ever, pressed the struggle for civil rights forward into the new opportunities he saw within the necessities created by the war and a nation increasingly tied together by a web of media.

Between 1940 and the advent of the cold war, the NAACP concentrated primarily on the integration of the armed forces and the defense industry, the representation and employment of African Americans in Hollywood, and the global drive toward anti-colonialism. All three issues were profoundly integrationist, and all three relied on the NAACP leveraging the demands of black America against the nation's need to defeat Germany and Japan. In the postwar realignment, though, White would have to make choices that would help split the global cause of black advancement. In the process he would prove a point Niebuhr had made in 1932 (and that White would have done well to heed): "If they [socialist leaders] are not more than usually honest their ambition will be tempted by the power and prestige which they may win as national rather than as proletarian leaders."

*

In January 1940, with Hitler massing his forces for the spring invasion of France and the Low Countries, there were five black officers in the regular army, three of them chaplains. Systematic segregation pervaded the defense industry and the armed forces, condoned by President Roosevelt and carried out by a military staffed disproportionately by Southerners. African Americans were not allowed in the Marines or the army air corps; in the navy they could serve only as messmen. So as war news arrived, many African Americans felt it wasn't their fight, instead welcoming any chance to see white folks wipe one another out. In 1917 Du Bois had rallied black America behind the flag, and the results, or lack thereof, were plain. This time America would have to offer more to its black citizens than empty promises if it expected them to help the war effort.

With 1940 an election year, there were indeed many promises—the Republican candidate Wendell Willkie made them in droves. A wealthy industrialist who'd tilted with FDR over the Tennessee Valley Authority project, Willkie was outspoken in his support for civil rights, anti-lynching legislation, and an end to Jim Crow everywhere, including the armed forces. Black newspapers, and increasing numbers of their readers, jumped on board the Willkie bandwagon, willing to end the New Deal coalition if it meant, among other things, the ability to serve in combat roles in the war that appeared on the horizon.

Willkie made many overtures to White for a meeting, all of which the secretary ignored, claiming the NAACP was apolitical while at the same time expressing his concerns to the first lady that the president needed to act quickly on desegregation or he'd lose the black vote. After no small wrangling, White, T. Arnold Hill of the National Youth Administration, and A. Phillip Randolph, the firebrand leader of the Brotherhood of Sleeping Car Porters, were allowed a meeting with FDR on September 27, 1940. There they demanded in no uncertain terms the complete integration of the defense industry and the armed forces. The president told Secretary of the Navy Frank Knox and Robert Patterson, assistant secretary of war, that black units were to be created in each branch and overall strategies developed for increased integration of forces. One idea he had was to station "a colored band on some of these ships, because they're darned good at it," a plan that White relates with no irony in his autobiography.

Once the black leaders had left the room, Knox threatened to resign if the president went through with what they'd just discussed. Two weeks later Steve Early, FDR's press secretary, released the War Department's new policy, which was essentially the same one it had had since 1937. It promised, among other things, black units in all branches but no integration. Worst of all, Early made it seem as if White, Randolph, and Hill had agreed to this. Embarrassed, all three reacted to the president's betrayal loudly, and with notes they'd taken that revealed FDR's dissembling. Not long after this, Steve Early kicked a black policeman in Harlem in the crotch for unknowingly blocking him from the president. The anti-FDR backlash was hot. As a sign of how out of touch Roosevelt was with black America, either by nature or by choice, he called in white Southerner Will Alexander to ask him what black voters wanted, even though three of their most august spokesmen had just told him. The result was a flurry of appointments, the most visible being Benjamin O. Davis to brigadier general and an old NAACP hand, William Hastie, to a post in the War Department.

Roosevelt carried the black vote in 1940, but it was really Willkie who lost the election. Avowedly internationalist, he had run on a platform of helping Britain face down Nazi Germany. As the election neared, however, the Republican candidate flip-flopped in dramatic fashion, suddenly taking an isolationist turn that questioned the veracity of his entire platform. Roosevelt held the White House easily, but whatever cordiality existed between FDR and White was gone. In 1943, when Arthur Spingarn asked the president for a letter of appreciation to honor White's twenty-five years with the NAACP, Roosevelt told his personal secretary to "tone it down" because he didn't "think too much of this organization."

Willkie and White, on the other hand, would go on to enjoy "one of the three or four closest and richest friendships" in White's life. The secretary sought Willkie out at a political dinner after the election and the two bluff, scotch drinkers hit it off immediately, both fond of grand pronouncements, neither as deep as they aspired to be, and both, in the end, a bit naive. Their mutual friends included Rebecca West and Willkie's lover, Irita Van Doren, wife of Carl Van Doren from the days of the Harlem Renaissance.

Surely White and Willkie had much to discuss, not the least of which was Willkie's new role as president of the board of Twentieth Century-Fox. After a decade spent wrangling with the White House and fighting rearguard actions within his own organization, White's short stint reviewing the script of *Gone with the Wind* had reignited his interest in the arts. "Whoever controls the film industry," Thomas Edison once said, "controls the most powerful medium of influence over the public"—a sentiment White now firmly agreed with. He had already been considering a Hollywood bureau of the NAACP that would act as an unofficial rating board, or censor, for black interests. Not long after his meeting with Willkie he would go west to try to heighten, not very successfully, attention to racism on and behind the screen. Until 1942 White would succeed in accomplishing three things in Hollywood: annoying the secretaries of producers with his incessant calls; insulting a generation of older black actors such as Hattie McDaniel and Stepin Fetchit, who made their livings portraying stereotypes; and having some smashing lunch dates with celebrities. But his new friendship with Willkie would soon bear fruit.

*

Sticking to the usual script, once elected FDR delivered on none of his promises to black America. By January 1941 a variety of organizations had begun to protest. The most intriguing idea came from A. Phillip Randolph, who called for a March on Washington on July 1 if the president did not order desegregation. White brought the NAACP very quickly on board this initiative, and while Randolph was the driver, the NAACP threw all its weight behind the movement, from national office down to branches. Formerly head of the National Negro Congress, Randolph had turned against the Communists and was among the black leaders White most respected.

Through the spring White worked on economic fronts, especially with labor leader Walter Reuther in building links between the NAACP and the CIO and lobbying for union-friendly legislation in Congress. When the United Auto Workers went on strike in Detroit, they asked the NAACP for help, and this time the organization stood solidly behind the strikers, confirming the close relationship the Detroit

branch had forged with the union. Meanwhile the momentum behind the March on Washington continued to build.
White delivered a fiery commencement address to the grad-
uating class at Fisk University, offering the White House no
quarter: black support for the coming war effort would require integration.

The idea of 100,000 African Americans marching on
Washington on July 1 scared the president about as much as
the empire of Japan. On June 10 the first lady sent a letter
asking that the march be called off. Eight days later, after ne-
gotiations with her and Fiorello La Guardia, mayor of New
York City, White and Randolph agreed to meet with FDR
to discuss their demands, a sweeping platform of changes
that would end discrimination in the military. The result of
their tense meeting was a landmark, Executive Order 8802,
which created the Fair Employment Practices Committee
to eliminate discrimination in the defense industry, signed
by FDR in July 1941, just after the Nazis invaded the Soviet Union. While it was a victory of sorts and welcomed
by most African Americans as a triumph, the FEPC fell well
short of what White and Randolph had asked for. FDR may
have already decided to create the FEPC beforehand, staging
the confrontation as a bit of political theater.

Not surprisingly, the White House did little else that
fall toward integrating the military. White suggested, with
wide support, that some voluntarily integrated units be created. Again the administration ignored him. Even so, White
was now unquestionably the nation's most prominent black
leader, and the achievement of Executive Order 8802 was a
result of his cooperation with another civil rights organization. Sharing the credit hadn't hurt the NAACP, though; instead membership swelled, with more than 150 new branches in 1941 and 1942, and the Legal Defense Fund continued
to pursue a slate of cases relating to education, with the first

lady's vocal support. Carl Van Vechten was back, wishing White "oak leaves and dahlias" as he gave his opinion on a proposed nude sculpture of James Weldon Johnson (happily, it was never made). And with the war edging closer and closer to American shores, White did not repeat Du Bois's mistake of suspending black demands until the fighting was over. Instead he continued to use black support of the war as a way to break down segregation. How, he asked, could Americans fight for democracy and justice overseas when it wasn't practiced at home?

After the Japanese bombed Pearl Harbor on December 7, 1941, the *Pittsburgh Courier*, riffing off of Churchill's victory sign, announced the Double V campaign to fight racism at home and abroad. With the nation charging as quickly as it could onto a war footing, and propaganda everywhere promoting unity, secrecy, and all other sorts of wartime virtue, White took the Double V to Hollywood, where, true to Edison's word, America looked more and more for its image and its meaning. Now, though, as part of the war effort, White wanted America to include a realistic image of its black citizens. In February 1942 White, Willkie, and producer Walter Wanger launched a nine-day assault on Hollywood.

On the surface White's trip west produced little other than hard feelings and some embarrassment. Working black actors (usually dark skinned) such as Hattie McDaniel, Willie Best, and Eddie Anderson, who played Jack Benny's servant Rochester, accused White, an Eastern intellectual with fair skin, of elitism and even a brand of racism. They conveniently ignored the fact that they made personal fortunes depicting characters that demeaned other African Americans and reinforced those images in the nation's psyche with every job. Despite overcoming their own challenges, the old-line black actors failed to see, or admit, that their time was over, and not just because Walter White said so. The nation, and especially the African-American community, was well ready for the honest inclusion of blacks in the content and creation of film, even as black Hollywood, so eager to accuse White of being self-serving and "white," continued to expend its time and energy saving itself.

Few producers would meet with White and Willkie on this first swing west, and when they did, White seemed more starstruck than militant. He even pitched a few script ideas. At the end, though, Willkie pulled together a final luncheon where White more eloquently stated his case to a roomful of studio executives, including Darryl Zanuck. All he asked was that they present "the Negro as a normal human being and integral part of human life and activity." Zanuck then stood up and said, "I never thought of this until you presented the facts."

Hollywood most likely would then have waved good riddance to White, except that the Roosevelt administration agreed with him and had opened a new Office of War Information (OWI) in Hollywood, charged in part with improving portrayals of blacks in film as an integral aspect of the war effort. As he continued to connect with Hollywood power brokers (and movie stars with big names he could drop into casual conversation), White met with OWI officials. Through the war years the OWI would, with the consultation of White and the NAACP, censor and guide black inclusion and portrayal on the screen. Changing the representation of an entire race was not a matter of flipping a switch or passing a law; White had to argue down to minutiae such as one black per ten whites in crowd scenes—he settled for one per fifteen. Then, once the moguls understood the importance of the work, the middle-level executives dug in.

The 1943 movie *Tennessee Johnson* was a test case of sorts. An MGM biopic of President Andrew Johnson, the movie as first shot portrayed Radical Reconstruction Senator Thaddeus Stevens in a particularly poor light, which set the Communist party agitating. Picking up the thread, both the OWI and White reviewed the script and pressured MGM into reshooting and recutting portions of the film. The result was a film admirable only in that it could have been worse. But the historian Thomas Cripps sees in this fight the seeds of something larger: the cooperation between the NAACP and the government "helped test a set of strategies of confrontation that would become a behavioral underpinning of the modern civil rights movement."

Many observers dismissed White's Hollywood forays as his "thing," a way to canoodle with the famous and stick a toe into movies with his script about Chadian president Felix Eboue, who had backed Free France in 1940 instead of throwing Africa to Hitler. Through 1946 White continued to consider a Hollywood bureau for the NAACP, which was finally established in 2003. But the long-term effect of his "thing" was profound. While the new image of black America on wartime screens was still a work in progress, in the name of the national good it was Walter White who ushered out the old one by balancing confrontation with cooperation.

*

Seeing a black extra in a crowd scene, though, was not enough to satisfy the needs of black Americans. Despite the advances made on paper, they still suffered discrimination at home and in the armed forces overseas. The denial of their role in defending their country equaled a denial of their right to their country itself. Even in the face of manpower shortages in Europe, the American military moved slowly if at all in sending black combat troops, employing them usually in labor and supply units. Anger festered at home and overseas. William Hastie, FDR's election sop, resigned from the War Department in protest. Finally, in 1943, the tension exploded into violence in Alabama, Detroit, and Harlem, first in May, when white workers at a Mobile shipyard rioted when black workers were given promotions, and then, weeks later, when whites at the Packard plant in Detroit called a wildcat strike because of the presence of black workers. The UAW stuck to its agreement with the NAACP and ordered the strikers back to their jobs, but in June the situation in Detroit turned violent at Belle Isle amusement park. Sporadic fighting between blacks and whites spiraled into a wave of attacks on blacks that included police participation.

White and Thurgood Marshall went to investigate, reporting that union cooperation was one of the elements that had kept the situation from turning into an all-out race riot. Things were so tense that White organized a national CBS radio broadcast on July 10 featuring a speech by Willkie urging calm and an end to discrimination. Its effect was slight, if any. On August 1, with Mussolini captured and American soldiers fighting their way across Sicily, Harlemites rampaged after an incident between a white policeman and a black soldier was twisted into rumors that the soldier had been killed. Commandeering a loudspeaker truck, White drove through the streets of Harlem informing rioters that the story wasn't true and begging them to return home.

*

Through the fall, the war in Europe became paramount as the Allies battled for control of Italy and Yugoslavia. Although no one could yet count on a total Allied victory, when it was all over, maps would be redrawn. Many hoped that power would be redistributed in a way that would finally offer the darker races of the world, not just African Americans, their fair share of the planet's wealth. In the previous five years White had driven a wedge into military discrimination and cultural misrepresentation, pushing against them with the weight of black America behind him. Now, from the time of the Normandy invasion through the creation of the United Nations and Harry Truman's election in 1948, White linked the struggle for civil rights to the global anti-colonial movement.

The first sign may have been his deep interest in the story of Felix Eboue, who as France fell made the decision to stand with Free France and thus keep West and Central Africa open to the Allies. Historians often point to this pet project of White's as evidence of both his craven desire to get into the movie business and his lack of critical judgment. But in fact the tale of the one man, a man of color, who stood between Hitler and world conquest was dramatic and timely, and Eboue, a brilliant progressive leader with a love of food and music, was sincerely a hero to White. The secretary's commitment to anti-colonialism was also sincere. He had been in Paris in 1919 with Du Bois at the second Pan-African Conference, but the pressing circumstances of black life in America had been more than enough for the NAACP to take on in the decades following. World War II, though, had shrunk the globe, giving "the Negro a sense of kinship with other colored—and also oppressed—peoples of the world," White wrote. He had loudly protested Churchill's statement that the 1941 Atlantic Charter espousing self-determination for all peoples did not apply to British colonies. When Indian nationalists refused to support the Allies unless Britain agreed to negotiate its independence, White joined the India League of America, signing a full-page *New York Times* ad in sympathy.

As usual, he had a personal angle on this too. His friend Willkie had topped the national best-seller lists in 1943 with *One World*, which told of his diplomatic trip around the world the year before, earning himself great reviews and big sales. White's plan now was to go to Europe in early 1944 on a fact-finding mission, send back articles for national magazines, and then write his own book about the experience, hopefully launching him into the role of celebrity intellectual that Willkie was now enjoying.

Fudging his letters of recommendation, White wrangled a three-month tour of the European theater, arriving unannounced in London in January 1944, to the displeasure of American officials, who feared he would stir up an already volatile situation, and the general puzzlement of the British. His book, *The Rising Wind*, describes the often smug responses he received from British officials, who bristled whenever he mentioned India and the end of the colonial system. Rather than shutting White out, though, they smothered him with kindness and cocktails, fobbing him off on lesser officials instead of granting his request for an audience with the king, and hoping the grandeur of the British Empire would distract him from its human cost.

Without question White enjoyed the fuss and color, and may not have played hard ball in his meetings, as if doing so would have melted the British colonial resolve. But he did know what he saw. Lady Astor greeted him by saying, "You *are* an idiot, . . . calling yourself a Negro when you're whiter than I am. . . ." As she jabbered on about their "good black boys" and her approval of segregation, White registered her as someone "convinced that control of the destinies of the world would remain in the hands of those who had held the reins before." Nor did he shirk from telling General Eisenhower what he thought of his acceptance of the racial status quo in the armed forces. Although admittedly awed by Ike, White mustered up the nerve to say that "while wars had to be fought and won, we must not fight them solely for the sake of making wars; that we had to change the patterns of thinking which caused men to fight." While in London he also met with Trinidadian Pan-African leader George Padmore to discuss the creation of a "world-wide colored liberation front composed of African, West Indians, Afro-Americans, and other colored races." White went on through Italy and North Africa, capping his journey with a visit to Eboue himself in Cairo, just before his death in May 1944.

*

White's return to New York took him off the global stage for the time being and put him back into politics, both national and within the NAACP. Admirable and attention-getting as his trip was, he'd left the organization without a functioning leader for almost six months, heading into another presidential election in the fall. No one questioned the message, but they did wonder about White's need to travel the world delivering it. The board now required him to stay in the country through at least the end of the year, hoping to diminish his taste for fame just a bit. His absence had also allowed others within the NAACP, such as Roy Wilkins, to build their own power bases that White would ultimately have to face down when his commitment to running the organization dipped below 100 percent. The years of unquestioned power for White were ebbing.

On a national level, Roosevelt prepared for another run for the White House and another dance with White. As the convention neared, FDR decided to replace his vice president, Henry Wallace. Secretary of Agriculture during the New Deal, Wallace had become a strong anti-colonialist with whom White found much common ground, but he was also perhaps the least conventional vice president the United States has ever had. A devotee of the painter and mystic Nicholas Roerich, Wallace had an earthy, spiritual bent rooted in his farm upbringing that, blended with causes of social justice and progressivism, had become a mystical mélange of

East and West, along the lines of Theosophy and the teachings of Gurdjieff. As Allied troops drove forward through France and the Netherlands, and postwar planning began, Wallace, who advocated a "people's revolution," would no longer be welcome on the ticket. Instead FDR floated the name of Senator James F. Byrnes—the same man who had pointed out White in the Senate gallery during the 1938 filibuster, who'd had no qualms about calling White a "nigger" on the record—as his next vice president. Not surprisingly, White launched a loud campaign, public and private, tearing into FDR for pushing aside Wallace, and bent on keeping Byrnes off the ticket. Eventually FDR relented, inserting Missouri senator Harry Truman instead. White crowed about another victory until the first lady sent him a quiet note pointing out that Truman had been FDR's choice all along, and White had merely played his part. Over the dissent of many within the organization and much of the black press, the NAACP stuck with the New Deal against Republican Thomas Dewey, securing Roosevelt his fourth term.

Turmoil was coming to the White home too. After their affair in the thirties, White and Poppy Cannon had gone their own ways. Cannon, on husband number three, was now an advertising executive. Following a brief encounter with Gladys one afternoon in New York, she invited White to lunch. "Somehow remote and middle-aged" (he was fifty-one), White now wore "steel-rimmed glasses which gave him a professorial look. His hair, which had been blond when I saw him last, was now almost white, and he was pounds heavier than he had been. The extra weight," she thought, "made him more attractive." Their affair resumed.

*

Although black combat troops played a significant role in winning the Battle of the Bulge, White's next trip abroad, to the Pacific theater, was a jolt. Unlike Europe, where the French and English were put off by American racism, Southern attitudes were given free rein in the South Pacific. White came home uncharacteristically discouraged, or at least slightly humbled. He could see that the work of the NAACP—*his* work—was part of a larger effort, a major realignment of global power that required a coalition of organizations across the ideological spectrum. With an Allied victory now just a matter of time, planning for the United Nations had begun at the Dumbarton Oaks meetings. Through the offices of Eleanor Roosevelt, the NAACP was named to consult on behalf of African Americans to the American delegation at the San Francisco UN Charter conference in April 1945.

By this point Du Bois had returned to the NAACP, at White's insistence, as director of special research, after a rancorous firing at Atlanta University. Although charged with adding some intellectual heft to the organization's international positions and connections, he also continued to work with Paul Robeson's Council on African Affairs (CAA) and other leftist groups, suspecting—rightly, as it would turn out—that the major powers, both political and corporate, who had won the war would have no interest in what the NAACP and other anti-colonial, international groups would have to say when the UN was built. To Du Bois's annoyance, White named himself leader of the NAACP delegation to the UN, over Du Bois and Mary McLeod Bethune, and gave a frenetic and for the most part superficial performance at the conference, providing window dressing for an American delegation only passingly concerned with the fate of billions of the world's darker citizens. For the anti-colonials, all that came of the conference were three paragraphs in the charter on the concept of trusteeship. Fought for by Ralph Bunche, now a member of the American delegation, they did set in

Lena Horne promotes the war effort, with White and Arthur Spingarn.
Horne was viewed with envy by many in Hollywood as White's special
protégé. *(Library of Congress)*

motion the gradual decolonization of the Third World, but
on a timetable so slow as to be unacceptable to the more
radical left.

Not all of White's attention was on the world stage. In
1945 Countee Cullen and Arna Bontemps teamed to write
a musical with music by Johnny Mercer and Harold Arlen.
Called *St. Louis Woman*, they wanted the beautiful young
black singer Lena Horne to star on Broadway and then in the
MGM film. When Horne, something of a project of White's,
was told by the secretary that the role envisioned for her,
that of a fallen woman, was a throwback to the stereotypes
he'd been fighting against in Hollywood with Willkie, she
pulled out. White was correct on all counts—the show and

the film both received mixed reviews at best and sank quickly. But Horne was not seen on Broadway for almost two decades after that, and Bontemps accused White of sabotaging the show to curry favor with another studio. The next year Disney's *Song of the South*, a sterilized, saccharine retelling of Joel Chandler Harris's Uncle Remus tales, featured James Baskett as Uncle Remus. So sweet in the role was Baskett that White's criticism of the film as retrograde and racist felt harsh, and after another round of trading barbs with the black acting establishment White eventually pulled back from Hollywood.

*

With the end of the war and FDR's death in the spring of 1945, new wars began, introducing new players and creating new alliances that would ultimately dictate where White would lead mainstream black activism. As Du Bois had feared, the winners were more interested in divvying up the spoils than dismantling anti-colonialism. After the San Francisco conference, White told President Truman of his disappointment with the UN charter and the role the United States was claiming in a new but still oppressive world structure. He loudly opposed further aid to Britain as long as it was used against colonial subjects, and he called Churchill's "Iron Curtain" speech "one of the most dangerous and cynical made in contemporary history by a presumably responsible man."

For all that, and the considerable faction of the left that wished to pacify the Soviet Union, decades of battling with and against Communists had given White a more realistic attitude toward them. Like many other liberals, he distrusted the Soviets even as he rejected the belligerent rhetoric of the right that suggested military action while the United States still held the nuclear advantage. When Paul Robeson, his old friend from the Harlem Renaissance, won the 1945 Spingarn Award, surely with White's blessing, the actor and activist delivered a pro-Soviet lecture. White, caught in the middle, blasted it in the press. A few months later he was back defending Robeson from attacks.

Love him or hate him, FDR had given America a kind of certainty with his long presidency, and that confidence wavered during Truman's first year in office. Critics accused the new president of lacking vision and direction—much as people had complained of White in the early thirties. Suspicions that Truman's Southern sympathies would reverse the New Deal seemed confirmed by a series of anti-labor and anti–civil rights decisions, capped in September by the firing of Henry Wallace as commerce secretary. The left began to lose patience. Among the Democrats, cracks appeared between progressives and centrists, including White, who were just as concerned that the New Deal stand but with a clear eye on the Soviets. And no one liked Truman.

As usual, White worked the fluid politics, decrying red-baiting and speaking out on behalf of Wallace along with Walter Reuther and the CIO as part of the Conference of Progressives. The same month he went to the Oval Office heading a group of civic, business, and religious leaders to demand at last some sort of anti-lynching protection. Truman expressed (most likely feigned) amazement when the facts surrounding a recent pair of lynchings were laid out, and insisted that something had to be done. Out of that meeting came the President's Committee on Civil Rights (PCCR), a plan it appears he had decided to enact before the meeting to shore up his black support. Through the fall of 1947 the PCCR worked on its report while the NAACP used the gathering momentum to initiate legislation on voting rights and other civil rights, and pursue its long struggle in the courts for educational rights through the Legal Defense Fund.

While the PCCR was a huge step forward, White remained unconvinced of Truman. He and Du Bois had begun fighting as soon as the *éminence grise* of the movement was back on board, but they agreed that the issue of domestic civil rights was still very much entwined with the anti-colonial movement that had all but stalled in the nascent UN. Never one to take things quietly, Du Bois received White's support to create a report, *An Appeal to the World*, which would state plainly and forcefully the place of the darker races in the world and their demands for fair and equal treatment. White pledged to help put it in play at the UN, but cold war politics, both global and domestic—as well as some of the personal sort—made him renege on that pledge. In doing so, he prompted a split in the American civil rights movement.

The schism among the Democrats became complete in the winter of 1946. That December leftist progressives rallied around Wallace. Then, in early January 1947, a group of anti-totalitarian progressives, formed during the war around the thought of Reinhold Niebuhr, reconfigured itself as the Americans for Democratic Action (ADA). Niebuhr's philosophy of ethical realism allowed a position that carried on the work of the New Deal, including strong support for civil rights, while standing in complete opposition to communism—a kind of muscular Christianity for the cold war. Along with Niebuhr, the ADA's members included Eleanor Roosevelt, embittered by her UN experiences with the Soviets, Walter Reuther, economist John Kenneth Galbraith, an actor-turned-activist named Ronald Reagan, and historian Arthur Schlesinger, Jr., who had warned in *Life* magazine of Communist infiltration of the NAACP. Joining Senator Hubert Humphrey and others on the organizing committee of twenty-six was Walter White.

In the ADA, with friends such as Roosevelt and Reuther at his side, White found a political home—and a philosophical one as well with Niebuhr, even if it was expressed only in how he did business. Joining ranks with Schlesinger also deflated the writer's dangerous charges about the NAACP, though soon the ADA would challenge the NAACP for White's loyalties. At the moment his other loyalties were being challenged. Thirty years of constant activity, scotch, and chain-smoking caught up to White in February, causing a heart attack. Sidelined for a few months, he took an office downtown, closer to the NAACP but far away from Gladys in Harlem. Sinclair Lewis's novel *Kingsblood Royal*, its mixed-race hero based in part on White, appeared to White's displeasure, chilling their friendship even as he and Poppy began to discuss a future together.

Outside, the cold war ratcheted up. The Communists took over Poland in January and made noises about Greece and Turkey, ringing alarms. At home, the House Un-American Activities Committee (HUAC) began ferreting out Communists in all walks of life. Fearing the spread of Communist influence, the administration now based its foreign policy on George Kennan's concept of containment, a strategy of countermoves to any Soviet political or military advance, which Truman announced in March 1947. In essence seconding Churchill's Iron Curtain speech, the Truman Doctrine accepted the leadership of the West from the British Empire, effectively blocking the anti-colonial cause.

The outlines of White's fateful choice now began to emerge. With the Democratic party falling apart, Truman tried to woo support from the ADA and black America by offering White more access to the White House. The president even closed the 1947 NAACP conference with a nationally broadcast speech from the steps of the Lincoln Memorial. Meanwhile *An Appeal to the World* and the increasingly fraught international agenda that Du Bois promoted in alliance with the Communists and the left now stood in counterpoise. That fall the PCCR delivered its report. Called *To*

White and Eleanor Roosevelt lead President Harry Truman to the Lincoln Memorial, where he's about to deliver the closing address to the 1947 NAACP convention. All four radio networks carried the speech; White claimed it "was by far the largest single audience in history to hear the story of the fight for freedom for the Negro in the United States." *(Yale Collection of American Literature, Beinecke Rare Book and Manuscript Library)*

Secure These Rights, it laid down a federal agenda for desegregation throughout the United States. While publicly supporting Du Bois and his ideas, and criticizing HUAC, White worked behind the scenes to delay the appearance of Du Bois's report, and even ordered him to help Eleanor Roosevelt on the rival Covenant on Human Rights for the UN. These actions allowed the release of *To Secure These Rights* to steal Du Bois's thunder. Considering White's many allegiances, it's likely that he did all this to quash Du Bois as much as to help Roosevelt and the ADA line in Washington. Du Bois and White were on the brink.

*

The year 1948 proved to be the climax of Walter White's life. The postman's son from Atlanta, Georgia; the former insurance salesman, agitator, and literary swell looked in the mirror each morning and saw a man tugging at the strings of global power as he strove to deliver his people to the Promised Land. How much that tugging actually produced is open to debate, and the names of the thousands who strove with him for civil rights are not fully known, but White looked to the fall of 1948 as a culmination of sorts. John Gunther called him one of the "64 men who run America." His daughter Jane, now graduated from Smith College, had debuted on Broadway in an adaptation of Lillian Smith's *Strange Fruit* and was doctoring the script of *Pinky* for Darryl Zanuck. In October, Viking would publish White's autobiography, *A Man Called White* (the title provided by Poppy). Other personal and professional changes were in store.

In the meantime the presidential election loomed in November. The combination of *To Secure These Rights* and the Truman Doctrine had rocked the Southern wing of the Democratic party. On February 2 the president addressed the nation to endorse the legislative agenda recommended by the PCCR. From the left, Wallace and the Progressive party prepared a run; in the South, Strom Thurmond led a Dixiecrat splinter party. Thomas E. Dewey, the Republican challenger, watched it all happily.

Despite the PCCR and Truman's address, Wallace with his pro–civil rights rhetoric was the obvious choice for most of black America as well as the NAACP, while White remained solidly in the ADA camp, which meant anti-Wallace. Even apart from Wallace's underwhelming civil rights record during the New Deal, for White to support the smallest faction of a fractured Democratic coalition—one with Communists in its ranks even as the Soviets blockaded Berlin—would produce nothing for black America, as Eleanor Roosevelt, now on the NAACP national board, surely pointed out.

Unhappy with Truman, the ADA reached out to Eisenhower and Supreme Court Justice William O. Douglas, until on the eve of the Democratic convention the organization finally came out for Truman. Senator Hubert Humphrey then orchestrated a battle for the first civil rights planks in the party platform, marking the ADA's first visible power play and giving White something to pay back. Soon after, Truman signed two landmark executive orders, one ending discrimination in federal employment and the other requiring equal opportunity in the armed forces. Once the ADA threw in behind Truman, White attacked Wallace full bore, regularly breaking NAACP rules on political partisanship in order to trumpet Truman in his column as he shut down in-house support for Wallace. Many in the organization, particularly Du Bois, who was very much a Wallace man, were furious. In early October, just as White prepared to leave for the next UN conference in Paris, Du Bois accused him of handing the NAACP over to Truman. While the president understood the value of NAACP backing and was ready to play politics for its support, it's closer to the truth to say that White had handed the NAACP over to Eleanor Roosevelt and the ADA.

Either way, Du Bois's charge was the last straw for White. After their falling out in the thirties, White had, in his unique fashion, still considered Du Bois a friend of sorts, handing out copies of Du Bois's *Black Reconstruction* to Eleanor Roosevelt and David O. Selznick, and advocating for him in various ways. But now all White saw were the politics involved and his inability to control the most influential voice in black America, while Du Bois saw little other than theory. Surely these were two trying men, neither of whom can be fully trusted when it comes to evaluating the other. Du Bois's depiction of these last years smacks of paranoia, with him as the innocent victim of White's scheming. White, of course, places all the blame on Du Bois and his ingratitude. The board fired Du Bois on the same day in September that White left for Paris to attend the UN General Assembly.

White had managed to place the NAACP within the heart of American power. Now, his health battered by three packs of cigarettes a day, his spirits lifted by his first great passion of the heart, and aligned with a movement made up of powerful, independent minds, White wanted to be more than just Mr. NAACP. He wanted to be Walter White, a pundit who transcended black and white. With his autobiography on the shelves, Du Bois out, and a new gig writing a weekly nationally syndicated column, White had one more announcement before he left for Paris: he would take a year's leave of absence as soon as he returned. On October 29 Harry Truman visited Harlem, the first American president ever to do so. A week later he was holding up the *Chicago Tribune*, beaming at a shocked nation, an upset winner mostly because of black votes.

*

The American delegation to the UN conference in Paris had one goal: to block any initiatives that came out of the Soviet Union. But the one delegate who argued the anti-colonial cause, a third path between communism and anti-Communist paranoia, was Walter White. Outgunned as he was, probably deluded as to his own meager influence on the proceedings, White continued to rally support for human rights, questioning containment and asking why the administration kept offering the moral high ground to the Soviets. But the days when he could tear into FDR and still expect favors were over. To shut him down, the administration accused White of sharing restricted information in a public briefing. Eleanor Roosevelt could not—or would not—bail him out. He was forced to compromise.

After three decades of work, White could see the goal ahead, and he was determined to lead his people forward to a desegregated America, no matter what. In order to keep his access to the Truman White House alongside the anti-Communist ADA, and maintain the NAACP in the vanguard of domestic civil rights, White no longer spoke out against American foreign policy, effectively severing the mainstream of black advocacy from the global struggle against colonialism. When he returned from Paris, White had a seat in Truman's inner circle, and he delayed his leave of absence to stay on through the legislative session. In the courts the Legal Defense Fund advanced in its educational cases. The cause of anti-colonialism fell to the far left.

Except no one had elected Walter White. The cause of global human rights suffered because he and Du Bois couldn't elevate their discourse beyond a squabble. Unable to articulate to black America the philosophical and theological motives that Niebuhr had given to postwar liberalism, ideas that posed a reasonable contrast to Du Boisian Marxism, White lost his mandate to lead. He was, after all, a salesman, and a fairly irreligious one at that. But because he was too busy moving pieces on the board to clarify, intellectually and emotionally, how he had positioned the NAACP within the tradition of Niebuhr, it would be left to a theologian, Dr. Martin Luther King, Jr., finally to express how these ideas informed black activism.

CHAPTER SEVEN

"I am white and I am black"

The Eightieth Congress resisted White's charms. That President Truman professed a commitment to civil rights far beyond FDR's altered the rhetoric on Capitol Hill and established a new moral benchmark on the issue. But that only meant that congressmen now expressed their regrets as they let civil rights legislation wither on the docket. The Truman Doctrine had legitimized Communist paranoia and now gave racism something new to hide behind: anyone who agitated too loudly for civil rights was branded a Red. White found his old lobbying skills coming up short. That spring it was time to effect all the changes in his life that he'd planned for the fall of '48.

The sense of expedience that allowed White to cut deals and keep moving had made many, mistakenly, see him as shallow or, worse, unprincipled. The reality was that White had never let principle stand in the way of achieving a principled goal. The ends, to Walter White, justified the means. That had been true back in his trickster days, scamming crackers down in Tennessee, and it was true as he worked the Oval Office and Senate chambers. What was most deceptive about White was the nature of his goals. He wanted to overthrow the tyrannies of racism and hunger and allow all Americans to pursue life, liberty, and happiness as they saw fit, but since he never indulged in the fantasy of revolution he gained the reputation of being an accommodationist. The truth is more nuanced.

Segregation had required a campaign of a thousand cuts, which bit by bit reduced the rights of African Americans; revoking it, he had understood, would involve the same process. And so White, longer than almost anyone else, kept his eyes on the prize, from the Margold Plan of legal challenges to segregation that had first stirred in 1925, now inching closer to *Brown v. Board of Education*, to forcing the arts honestly and fully to depict African Americans in every new media that came along. Always seeing that goal, always looking into a future where race would matter but not ultimately determine where you worked, where you lived, and who you married, made White in many ways ahead of his time. It's why his last years defy simple description as tragic, bittersweet, or a betrayal. Today White's last act—personal and professional—would at most raise a few eyebrows, last a news cycle or two, before attention moved on. But in 1949 they cost him his place in history.

*

While it's not clear that White had set a specific time with Poppy for leaving Gladys, knowing what it would mean and how dramatically it would alter his life must have kept him from doing it sooner. He sent mooning letters to Poppy when he wasn't stealing time with her, talked about a future together, until in February 1949 he took an unseemly angle of escape by accusing Gladys of having an affair (Fredric March, the actor, was a name in play). By now Gladys must have heard rumors of her own, and though she protested vehemently she finally agreed to a divorce. Few were surprised; it had been a loveless marriage of two people ill-suited to be parents, resulting in twenty-five silent, oppressive years in the White home.

Gladys White (center) speaks with her daughter Jane, as Walter appears to be elsewhere in this staged shot from the late 1940s. *(Yale Collection of American Literature, Beinecke Rare Book and Manuscript Library)*

Now White meant to be shed of more. In April he told the NAACP board that the public affairs radio show *Town Meeting of the Air* had invited him to join a distinguished group touring the world, broadcasting question-and-answer sessions with local audiences. When the board did not immediately grant him leave—and the required expense money—White simply announced that effective June 1 he would resign his post at the NAACP. No one was ready for him to leave, even Roy Wilkins, who had been complaining about his boss for decades now. Either White had so dominated him that after eighteen years as the number two Wilkins lacked the confidence to step up, or Wilkins had been talking through his hat. Begged to reconsider, White agreed to wait until he returned a year later to decide whether this departure was final.

And yet this wasn't the bombshell. To most outside observers, it was time for White to step aside. Even though he enjoyed private policy dinners with the ADA's Humphrey, Joseph Rau, and Truman's right-hand man Clark Clifford, he was ready to become the national pundit he'd been positioning himself as on radio, TV, and in print. No, what stunned the world was White's marriage to Poppy Cannon in Jersey City on July 6, 1949. As soon as the knot was tied, the newlyweds were off to London to join the *Town Meeting* cast, leaving the shrapnel to settle over what was left of White's legacy.

Love does not know color—Frederick Douglass's second wife had been white; Du Bois, hardly a model husband and father himself, had been in love with a white *Fräulein* during his years in Germany—but White's timing couldn't have been worse. To be as fair skinned as White was, to have survived challenges made because people suspected he actually was white, to have negotiated and compromised with the white power structure in such a way that the goals of African Americans were carved away from the global anti-colonial struggle—and then to marry a white woman? That was more than the black community could tolerate. Every question, suspicion, and qualm ever held against him—and there were many—now came roaring out. He had always wanted to be white, said some; he always *had* been white, said others.

As White and his new wife traveled the world largely oblivious to the furor at home, chatting with Nehru and General MacArthur among others, the black press tore into him. The NAACP was thrown into confusion, many on the board calling for his immediate dismissal. Friends and family chose sides, but those who felt angry, betrayed, and hurt far outnumbered supporters. White's sisters delivered the harshest judgments, echoing the accusations of others that he'd wanted all along simply to pass as Caucasian. His ex-wife and children broke off with him; Pidge changed his name from Walter White, Jr., to Carl Darrow.

Any hopes of cooler heads prevailing disappeared in August when *Look* magazine ran an article by White titled "Has Science Conquered the Color Line?" In it he describes an alleged scientific breakthrough, a skin-lightening chemical that will eliminate the color line once and for all by letting everyone be white. White's choice of wife was now more than a matter of love; he himself had thrown it against a puzzling backdrop of confused racial identity that he'd always seemed to master. From now on White would never again be seen in the same way by black America. By describing whiteness as a solution, as something to be aspired to, he profoundly insulted the people he'd given his life to and all but destroyed his own enormous legacy.

When he and Poppy returned in the fall, White mounted a lame defense. It had been satire, he claimed, like his friend George Schuyler's *Black No More*, the 1935 novel in which a formula is discovered that lets black people turn white. Since the last pages of *A Man Called White* touch on the same idea—"Suppose the skin of every Negro in America were suddenly to turn white," he asks—but as a hypothetical, most likely this was less a revelation of his true desires than a clumsy extension of that quasi-philosophical, undergraduate question. Once again White defines blackness as who he is, which in this case is someone who defines himself beyond race. Even within the context of anti-colonialism and his solidarity with dark races around the world, White wanted individual character to matter more than skin color. He wanted black people of all skin tones to realize the full range of possibilities within themselves and not just exercise the easy politics of race. "There are Negro capitalists and Negro paupers," he writes in *A Man Called White*, "Negro Republicans, Democrats, Socialists, and Communists; there are Negro internationalists and Negro chauvinists. I have always strongly advocated that in a

democracy Negroes should function as members of a democratic society and not as a segregated bloc." He wanted justice and opportunity and access to resources applied evenly,
every man judged, just as King would say, "not by the color
of their skin, but by the content of their character." As positive and hopeful as White's vision of a color-blind world
was, his bizarre expression of it in *Look* lacked the simple
grace and depth of Dr. King's words. If rather than a world of
all white he had imagined a world of all orange or green, he
would have been closer to the ideal he had given his life to.
Instead he sullied what he stood for and undercut his own
ambitions as a mass-media figure.

Still officially on leave of absence, White continued writing his column, planning a television show, making speeches, and the like. His public comments tend to be cold war
updates of the Double V approach of World War II: fighting
fascism had required fighting racism, and now that was true
in places such as India, where food assistance, he told Truman, would block Soviet influence. Events of the last six
months had poisoned his relationship with the NAACP. Even
as he tried to step out, he touted his resumé and connections, as if unsure whether he'd be accepted on his own, and
to some degree his concern was well founded. His relation
to a mainstream organization had made his nationally syndicated column possible. Perhaps it was necessary: Poppy
Cannon felt that the *New York Herald Tribune* dropped him
in 1950 for weighing in on too wide a range of issues. Fifty
years later the job he coveted as a talking head would have
been his for the asking—Walter White would have loved
cable television and the internet.

Losing the *Herald Tribune*, though, punctured his dream
of national celebrity and lowered his value, such as it was, in
the political realm. Without the power of the NAACP beneath
him and no major outlet for his writing, he would become

simply a politician without a constituency. So in March 1950 he apprised the board of his intention to return to the NAACP, news that was not well received. Roy Wilkins, who had finally stepped up to the leadership position, lined up against him. Eleanor Roosevelt threatened to quit the board if White was not brought back, a possible PR disaster for the organization. Clearly, keeping the NAACP in the ADA family was crucial. The board drifted, unsure of what it wanted to do until finally William Hastie took things in hand and helped craft the solution that probably would have best served everyone a year earlier. With so much changing in the world and in the organization, the NAACP had been examining a reorganization, and now it was time to implement it. After a long and difficult meeting, the result was White as executive secretary, a figurehead job, and Wilkins as day-to-day administrator. The board tried to prevent White from doing any more writing outside his job, but he successfully fought that, pointing out the public relations value of all he had done over the years. Besides, he needed the money.

*

Although Walter White remained at the top of the NAACP letterhead, his leadership of the organization was effectively ended. He spoke out, to the annoyance of many, against the report *We Charge Genocide*, presented to the UN as proof of the global oppression of people of color, claiming it was essentially Communist propaganda that offered an incomplete view of racial progress. With Du Bois and Robeson both jailed for their political beliefs in 1951, White chose to thrust himself into the middle of an irrelevant fight between the Stork Club and famed performer Josephine Baker, who claimed that she'd been ill-served because she was black. By the end of that year Mary White Ovington, Charles Houston, and Louis T. Wright had all died.

Yet White's last years were not unhappy, or unhinged. A progression of heart attacks in 1952 made it clear that he did not have much time left, but living between midtown and Poppy's home in Connecticut, White received rounds of important figures. The son of a man so resolutely Congregationalist must have felt comfortable finally living on stony Connecticut ground. Although he would never repair his relationships with his son and daughter, White managed to stitch himself back into the lives of his sisters, trading visits with them and their families, and even catching up with Norris Herndon, the millionaire heir to Alonzo's insurance fortune, and Lucy Rucker. Too buttoned up ever to express what pain the loss of his children must have caused, White showed some understanding of what he hadn't done with them by dispensing creaky but well-intended stepfatherly advice to Poppy's children Claudine and Alf, evidencing the patience he'd never had with Jane and Pidge. He and Poppy rarely left each other's sight. With his second wife, White, as powerful men seem to do, found unqualified devotion for the man he'd made of himself.

Marginalized by now, White enjoyed a last hurrah in May 1954 when the Supreme Court announced its verdict in *Brown v. Board of Education*. Thurgood Marshall had long been directing the course of the Legal Defense Fund, but White commandeered the microphone at the press conference to make sure that some of the spotlight fell on him, upsetting the future Supreme Court justice who'd had no time for White after his remarriage. It was a view of Canaan for a flawed Moses.

*

Five months later White suffered a massive coronary. Although invited as the only American to the conference of nonaligned nations in the summer of 1955, he had to refuse and instead worked on his last book, *How Far the Promised*

Land, a state of the union of sorts for black America, published after his death. Read as a snapshot of black life, it is overly optimistic, but it was White's final summation and a passing of the hammer to a new generation.

On March 21, 1955, Walter White died in his midtown apartment from yet another heart attack. Thousands lined the streets of Harlem, and tribunes came from around the world, from President Eisenhower and foreign leaders. Even Paul Robeson attended the funeral. The *New York Times* called him "the nearest approach to a national leader of American Negroes since Booker T. Washington," and the black press to a newspaper mourned him without qualification. He was a spokesman, said the *Chicago Defender,* "for all Americans who loved justice and for the great majority of the world's peoples who are colored."

Almost nine months after White's death, on December 1, 1955, a seamstress and former secretary of the Montgomery, Alabama, branch of the NAACP named Rosa Parks refused to give up her seat on a city bus to a white man. Another page was turned, and the modern civil rights movement continued a struggle fought by generations of men and women before it. Roy Wilkins now had the run of the NAACP, and though Dr. Martin Luther King, Jr., would quickly eclipse him, Wilkins, with Thurgood Marshall and other veterans of years of NAACP infighting, all but erased White from the record, eager to put their own stamp on the organization. The photo in *Jet* magazine of Emmett Till's mutilated body began a parade of painful, unforgettable images from places such as Birmingham and Selma. Dr. King's speech at the March on Washington and burning buses on the highways of the South buried the memory of a complex man of ambiguous color who had risked as much as any Freedom Rider, and many times over. If he was discussed at all, it was in terms of accommodation and skin color, as someone who hadn't betrayed his people really, because he'd never actually been black in the first place. Walter White was not just written out of history; he was stripped of his race.

Some might say he'd have been happy about that. Few men have had less illusions about the importance of skin color than Walter White. "I am white and I am black," is how he closes his autobiography, "and know that there is no difference. Each casts a shadow, and all shadows are dark." But by defining blackness in a broad, almost philosophical way, in a way that stressed values rather than skin, White had always considered himself black. And he'd done more than philosophize; few surpassed his actions. He'd been that baby in Atlanta when Booker T. Washington had waved his flag of surrender to segregation, walked alone down rural streets after lynchings, willingly risking his life for civil rights. When few believed it was worth it in the face of the depression, White had fought to keep the NAACP on the path of the Margold Plan, to pursue educational court cases. *Brown v. Board of Education* was the product of his vision of the NAACP and of civil rights. As District Court Judge John Parker sought to reduce the power of the *Brown* decision over the next few years, it proved that if Parker had indeed risen to the bench in 1930, *Brown* would have gone another way. The results were a changed world.

In the end, White's story is a riff on the American Dream: a young salesman armed with the gift of gab, courage, and a ferocious energy confounds the hard odds of his upbringing to reach a pinnacle of success. But those stories don't often end well, especially when politics come into play, where even the best and the brightest must stop occasionally to scrape off the moral barnacles that gather. If White had not followed the road not taken and gone straight into business, he could very well have been a titan. His commitment and vision, his charming megalomania, had all the marks of a corporate

Roy Wilkins (left) would succeed White as secretary of the NAACP while Thurgood Marshall (right) would go from directing the Legal Defense Fund to the Supreme Court. *(Library of Congress)*

CEO, a man who could make the world spin around him. But White, a man of enormous self-regard, instead walked knowingly onto a path that demanded humility. That he tried many times to get out, to begin new careers related to civil rights, ones not requiring sacrifice, shows that he was not always comfortable in the place he'd found himself. Yet by the time James Weldon Johnson left the NAACP, White's other avenues to success had either closed or been proven dry wells. Like it or not, he was now one with his cause, with the NAACP, and the result was an unstoppable passion to help his race, woven with the threads of his own ambition and a pragmatic philosophy.

With the departure of Du Bois in the mid-1930s, White controlled the agenda of the NAACP, leading it in directions that would ultimately bear fruit in many, many ways. White was not a religious man, nor was he a dreamer. Foolish as he thought racism was, he had no fantasies of worldwide epiphany any more than he believed in revolution. What had to change were the laws, the details, the facts of daily life that allowed a man to earn a living, raise a family, and dream of a future. By the time of White's death, Robeson and Du Bois had embraced Stalinism, and Abram Harris, once a leftist, had gone on to the University of Chicago, where he helped grow the conservative Chicago school of economics that gave the world Milton Friedman. George Schuyler eventually courted the John Birch Society. And yet Walter White, a man of few theories and many tactics, remained squarely, sanely, and consistently down the middle for almost four decades. This was hardly a dramatic or even an inspiring legacy when not dressed in Niebuhr's robes, but it displayed a deep understanding of the American system and the flaws and glory of its people. For better or worse, White left this world seeing not a black man or a white man in the mirror but a human being.

It is Niebuhr, finally, who offers the most penetrating judgment of White. In *Moral Man and Immoral Society*, he writes, "No political realism which emphasizes the inevitability and necessity of a social struggle, can absolve individuals of the obligation to check their own egoism, to comprehend the interests of others and thus to enlarge the areas of co-operation." The idealism of being color-blind, of seeing oneself as an individual above all other identities of class and color, brings hazards of its own. Tragically, for all his passionate risk-taking, his political savvy and commitment to the cause, Walter White came to serve his own ego above everything else. In his drive to give every man and woman their individual rights, and to take the credit for it, he undercut the racial unity and strength that could possibly have brought those rights even sooner, sadly clouding a legacy that we should otherwise celebrate.

Acknowledgments

MY THANKS, first, to Professor John David Smith, who not only commissioned this book but also took a great chance on me. I hope he finds his confidence rewarded. Ivan Dee has been a thoughtful editor and a supportive, creative publisher throughout the process, while Walter Vatter has gone over and above the assignment. They are two gentlemen of the old school, and I deeply appreciate that. My thanks and admiration also go to Professor Kenneth Janken for his friendship and his intellectual openness, as well as to Sondra Wilson and Jon-Christian Suggs.

When I first began researching the life of Walter White, Adriana Trigiani and especially Susan Fales-Hill lit the way; they're truly the godmothers of this book. White's niece, Rose Palmer, has generously shared her time and thoughts with me, adding significantly to my work. Most of all, though, Jane White Viazzi has given me years of honesty, candor, and insight into her father's life. Her trust charged me with recreating more than just the fact of White's life but a sense of who he was as a man. My debt to her is significant.

And, of course, to my wife Suzanne and my children Nick and Kaye. In the end, all my books are for them.

A Note on Sources

ANY STUDY of Walter White must begin with Kenneth Janken's *White: The Biography of Walter White, Mr. NAACP* (New York, 2003), the most complete biography to date and exhaustive when it comes to the inner machinations of the NAACP during this period. While Professor Janken and I disagree on certain motivations and conclusions, his scholarship is impeccable; it informs this book throughout. Aside from White's own writings—*Fire in the Flint* (New York, 1924), *Flight* (New York, 1926), *Rope and Faggot: A Biography of Judge Lynch* (New York, 1929), *A Rising Wind* (Garden City, 1945), *A Man Called White* (New York, 1948), and *How Far the Promised Land?* (New York, 1955)—Robert Zangrando's *The NAACP Crusade Against Lynching, 1909–1950* (Philadelphia, 1980) and Charles Flint Kellogg's *NAACP: A History of the National Association for the Advancement of Colored People* (Baltimore, 1967) provide the broad context for White's story and should come at the beginning of any further reading in his life. Manfred Berg's *"The Ticket to Freedom": The NAACP and the Struggle for Black Political Integration* can also serve as an excellent general introduction to the organization and its history.

For this brief biography I have also consulted the NAACP papers in the Library of Congress; the Beinecke Library at Yale University; the Schomburg Collection and the Joel Spingarn Collection, both at the New York Public Library; the Clark Atlanta University Library; the Auburn Avenue branch of the Atlanta Public Library; and the Oral History collection at Columbia University.

Chapters One and Two

Segregation cannot be fully appreciated without an understanding of Reconstruction, and Eric Foner's *Reconstruction* (New York, 1988) is the basic text on that subject. John Dittmer's *Black Georgia in the Progressive Era, 1900–1920* (Urbana, 1977), Mark Bauerlein's *Negrophobia: A Race Riot in Atlanta, 1906* (San Francisco, 2001), Carole Merritt's *The Herndons: An American Family* (Athens, Ga., 2002), Gary Pomerantz's popular *Where Peachtree Meets Sweet Auburn* (New York, 1996), and Alexa Benson Henderson's *Atlanta Life Insurance Company: Guardian of Black Economic Dignity* (Tuscaloosa, 1990) all provide valuable insights into the city and times White grew up in, with *Black Atlanta in the Roaring Twenties* (Charleston, 1997) by Herman "Skip" Mason, Jr., offering a photographic record. The works of Pete Daniel—*The Shadow of Slavery: Peonage in the South 1901–1969* (Urbana, 1972) and *Standing at the Crossroads: Southern Life Since 1900* (New York, 1986)—are especially illuminating about the South before World War I. *The Strange Career of Jim Crow* (New York, 1955) by C. Vann Woodward and *The Story of John Hope* (New York, 1948) by Ridgely Torrence are two important books well worth the time of any general reader. Finally, for an unusual insight into Atlanta's fair-skinned African-American community, *Harvard African Studies, vol. X* (Cambridge, 1932), contains a study by Du Bois's student Caroline Bond Day that includes family trees and photographs. It's anthropology done with rough tools, but intriguing all the same.

The letters of James Weldon Johnson quoted in this chapter came from the James Weldon Johnson Papers, James Weldon Johnson Collection in the Yale Collection of American Literature, Beinecke Rare Book and Manuscript Library.

Chapter Three

For thoughts regarding White as a trickster, I owe a great debt to Lewis Hyde's *Trickster Makes This World* (New York, 1998) and Henry Louis Gates's seminal *The Signifying Monkey* (New York, 1988). Both books are the kind that change the way we see the world, or at least they've changed mine. Further reading on black linguistic traditions should begin with Geneva Smitherman's

Talkin and Testifyin: The Language of Black America (Detroit, 1977). The early linguistic work of Roger O. Abrahams, in books such as *Positively Black* (Englewood Cliffs, N.J., 1970) and *Talking Black* (Rowley, Mass., 1976), creaks a bit today, but his collection of African-American folklore, *African-American Folktales* (New York, 1999), stands shoulders above the rest. *Black Culture and Black Consciousness* by Lawrence W. Levine (New York, 1977) makes for a fine starting point here as well.

Along with Zangrando and Kellogg, the NAACP as White came to it is well-documented by James Weldon Johnson in his autobiography *Along This Way* (New York, 2000), Mary White Ovington's *Black and White Sat Down Together: The Reminiscenes of an NAACP Founder* (New York, 1995), Carolyn Wedin's *Inheritors of the Spirit: Mary White Ovington and the Founding of the NAACP* (New York, 1998), and Du Bois's own *Autobiography* (New York, 1968). David Levering Lewis's Pulitzer Prize–winning biography *W. E. B. Du Bois: Biography of a Race, 1868–1919* (New York, 1993) and *W. E. B. Du Bois: The Fight for Equality and the American Century: 1919–1963* (New York, 2000), is brilliantly written and a model of history that's both academically sound and open to the general reader. Quotations of letters from Mary White Ovington to Joel Spingarn come from the Joel E. Spingarn Papers, Manuscripts and Archives Division, New York Public Library; Astor, Lenox and Tilden Foundation

Details on the Red Summer of 1919 may be found in Arthur Waskow's *From Race Riot to Sit-In* (Garden City, N.Y., 1966), Eliot Asinof's *1919: America's Loss of Innocence* (New York, 1990), and, best of all, *Race Riot: Chicago in the Red Summer of 1919* (New York, 1970) by William M. Tuttle, Jr. Readings on the Chicago riot should also include *The Chicago Race Riots* by Carl Sandburg (New York, 1919) and *The Negro in Chicago* (Chicago, 1922), edited by Charles Johnson of Urban League fame. *Blood in Their Eyes: The Elaine Race Massacres of 1919* (Fayetteville, Ark., 2001) by Grif Stockley is the one volume devoted to the entire Elaine case, though Stockley's view of White is in my opinion overly negative, especially when compared to his praise for Scipio Jones. *"We Return Fighting": The Civil Rights Movement in the Jazz Age* (Boston, 2002) by Mark Robert Schneider is also particularly insightful about this period and up through the 1920s, and sheds light on White's involvement in the Aiken, South Carolina, case.

The literature on lynching is deep, but Stewart Tolnay and E. M. Beck's *A Festival of Violence: An Analysis of Southern Lynching, 1882–1930* (Urbana, 1995) is probably the best historical analysis. In the end the authors are forced to admit that White's conclusions in *Rope and Faggot* were generally on point. Arthur Raper's *The Tragedy of Lynching* (Chapel Hill, 1933) is worth review, as is the chapter on James Weldon Johnson in Jacqueline Goldsby's *A Spectacular Secret: Lynching in American Life and Literature* (Chicago, 2006) and, of course, *Southern Horrors and Other Writings: The Anti-Lynching Campaign of Ida B. Wells, 1892–1900* (Boston, 1997), a collection of Ida B. Wells's groundbreaking writings on this topic, edited by Jacqueline Jones Royster.

Chapter Four

Anyone interested in the Harlem Renaissance should begin with David Levering Lewis's *When Harlem Was in Vogue* (New York, 1981). Especially of interest is Lewis's brief portrait of White, which stands as the best quick sketch. Edward Waldron's *Walter White and the Harlem Renaissance* (Port Washington, N.Y., 1978) offers only a limited picture of White, but it covers well the difficult publication of *Fire in the Flint* and gives White the novelist a fair hearing. While there are now shelves of books about the Harlem Renaissance, it's disturbing how many of them ignore White, get the facts wrong, or present a view of the period based more on received wisdom and fashion than on real history. For a crisply written and beautiful visual record, see Carole Marks and Diana Edkins, *The Power of Pride: Stylemakers and Rulebreakers of the Harlem Renaisssance* (New York, 1999), and Allon Schoener's *Harlem on My Mind: Cultural Capital of Black America, 1900–1968* (New York, 1968). The recent volume by George Hutchinson, *In Search of Nella Larsen: A Biography of the Color Line* (Cambridge, Mass., 2006), portrays the time with the complexity it deserves. Mr. Hutchinson also edited *The Cambridge Companion to the Harlem Renaissance* (Cambridge, Mass., 2007). *The New Negro*, edited by Alain Locke (New York, 1925), is the most important set of primary documents on the period. The letters of Carl Van Vechten (New Haven, 1987) offer a look at a fascinating raconteur and more over-the-top ways to close a letter than a reasonable person could ever imagine. For Von Vechten's later characterizations of

White, see "Reminiscences of Carl Von Vechten" (October 1960), on pages 20, 195, 266, 270, and 272 in the Columbia University Oral History Research Office Collection. Kevin Boyle's award-winning *Arc of Justice: A Saga of Race, Civil Rights, and Murder in the Jazz Age* (New York, 2004) covers the Ossian Sweet case with the right combination of verve and scholarship.

Chapter Five

For the Parker confirmation battle, see Kenneth W. Goings's *"The* NAACP *Comes of Age": The Defeat of Judge John J. Parker* (Bloomington, Ind., 1990). *The Selling of Supreme Court Nominees* by John Anthony Maltese (Baltimore, 1995) was also helpful in placing the struggle in context. Valuable titles on civil rights in the 1930s include *Speak Now Against the Day: The Generation Before the Civil Rights Movement in the South* (Chapel Hill, 1994) by John Edgerton, *Making Whiteness: The Culture of Segregation in the South, 1890–1940* (New York, 1998) by Grace Elizabeth Hale, Dan T. Carter's *Scottsboro: A Tragedy of the American South* (Baton Rouge, 1976), and James Goodman's more narrative *Stories of Scottsboro* (New York, 1994).

The literature on the depression, the New Deal, and the Roosevelt presidency takes up many feet of shelf space. Arthur Schlesinger's three-volume history of the New Deal—*The Crisis of the Old Order* (Boston, 1957), *The Coming of the New Deal* (Boston, 1958), and *The Politics of Upheaval* (Boston, 1960)—is almost a kind of autobiography, told as it is by a committed New Dealer. *F.D.R. and the South* (Baton Rouge, 1965) by Frank Freidel puts a finer edge on President Roosevelt's situation regarding Southern support for the New Deal, while John B. Kirby's *Black Americans in the Roosevelt Era* (Knoxville, 1980) and Harvard Sitkoff's *A New Deal for Blacks* (New York, 1978) both present in great detail the challenges and advances of African Americans under FDR. For insight on the first lady, I relied on Blanche Wiesen Cook, especially the second volume of *Eleanor Roosevelt: 1933–1938* (New York, 1992). Reinhold Niebuhr's *Christianity and Power Politics* (New York, 1940) and especially *Moral Man and Immoral Society* (New York, 1932) should be read by every thinking member of society.

For the inner workings of the NAACP during this time, start with Sondra Kathryn Wilson's *In Search of Democracy: The*

NAACP *Writings of James Weldon Johnson, Walter White and Roy Wilkins, 1920–1977* (New York, 1999) as a collection of White's writings not just in this decade but on both sides of it. Also consult Roy Wilkins's autobiography *Standing Fast* (New York, 1982), Eugene D. Levy's *James Weldon Johnson: Black Leader, Black Voice* (Chicago, 1973), and Raymond Wolters's *Du Bois and His Rivals* (Columbia, Mo., 2002).

Chapters Six and Seven

I found Penny Von Eschen's *Race Against Empire: Black Americans and Anticolonialism, 1937–1957* (Ithaca, 1997) and Steven M. Gillon's *Politics and Vision: The ADA and American Liberalism, 1947–1985* (New York, 1987) most useful in placing White in context post–World War II, both internationally and domestically. There is room for a deeper inquiry into White's relationship with the ADA and its impact on the civil rights movement. The biographies *Ralph Bunche: An American Life* (New York, 1993) by the distinguished Brian Urquhart, and *Dark Horse: A Biography of Wendell Willkie* (Garden City, N.Y., 1984) by Steve Neal were also of great value. *Slow Fade to Black: The Negro in American Film, 1900–1942* (New York, 1977) and *Making Movies Black: The Hollywood Message Movie from World War II to the Civil Rights Era* (New York, 1993), both by Thomas Cripps, made for some of my most enjoyable reading during my research. They're thoroughly engaging, rich in anecdote, and broad of vision. *Black Images in the American Theatre* (Brooklyn, 1973) is idiosyncratic but ultimately very useful in laying out the NAACP's participation in the arts. Richard Dalfiume's *Desegregation of the U.S. Armed Forces* (Columbia, Mo., 1969) is definitive on this topic. Finally, Poppy Cannon's book, *A Gentle Knight: My Husband, Walter White* (Viking, 1956) is more of a curiosity than a truly reliable source; so much is factually askew that one begins to question the entire effort, but what is clear is that she loved the man beyond the quality of her words. Although hagiography, it gives an impression of the later White if not a factual record.

Index

A NOTE ON THE AUTHOR

Thomas Dyja was born in Chicago and studied at Columbia University. He has been a bookseller and a book editor, and now devotes his time entirely to writing. His other books include three novels— *Play for a Kingdom*, *Meet John Trow*, and *The Moon in Our Hands*—and, with Dr. Rudy Crew, *Only Connect: The Way to Save Our Schools*. He has also edited five anthologies. He lives in New York City with his wife and two children.